BEYOND AUTHORITY

LEADERSHIP IN A CHANGING WORLD

Julia Middleton

First published 2007 by
PALGRAVE MACMILLAN

Palgrave Macmillan in the UK is an imprint of Macmillan Publishers Limited, registered in England, company number 785998, of Houndmills, Basingstoke, Hampshire RG21 6XS.

Palgrave Macmillan in the US is a division of St Martin's Press LLC, 175 Fifth Avenue, New York, NY 10010.

Palgrave Macmillan is the global academic imprint of the above companies and has companies and representatives throughout the world.

Palgrave® and Macmillan® are registered trademarks in the United States, the United Kingdom, Europe and other countries.

ISBN-13: 978-0-230-50001-3
ISBN-10: 0-230–50001-3

This book is printed on paper suitable for recycling and made from fully managed and sustained forest sources. Logging, pulping and manufacturing processes are expected to conform to the environmental regulations of the country of origin.

A catalogue record for this book is available from the British Library.

A catalog record for this book is available from the Library of Congress.

2006047144

11
17   16   15   14   13   12

Printed and bound in Great Britain by
CPI Antony Rowe, Chippenham and Eastbourne

About the author

Julia Middleton is Chief Executive of Common Purpose, which she founded in 1989.

Common Purpose runs unique, community-based leadership development programs (described as a "street-smart MBA") in over 50 cities in the UK and in many cities in Europe, Africa, and India.

Julia lives with her husband and five children in London.

Contents

Foreword

It happens again and again. Bright, aggressive managers move quickly up an organization and then, quite suddenly, find themselves becalmed. The skills that seemed to be serving them so well are just not enough. We have all seen the heads shake. He, or she, is *"not very good with people"* or *"doesn't seem able to see the wood for the trees"* or *"is not very good at lateral thinking."*

We know what this really means. They may be great, but somehow they are not quite leaders. Someone once said that there are actually three kinds of people: leaf people who just see leaves, tree people who see leaves and trees, and far more rarely, forest people who understand that leaves and trees make up forests and that forests are very different.

Julia is a forest person. And her book is about what makes forest people, why they matter more than ever, and what it takes to become one. Of course, such people are as old as time. How did Hannibal lead so many people – and elephants – over such long distances without even one laptop to help him? What made Wilberforce able to persuade so many thousands that slavery was not simply morally odious, but that it should be abolished? Why has Nelson Mandela not exacted terrible revenge from those who imprisoned him? How come John Lewis had an idea for a "non-capitalist" company that still works today – in the most intensely competitive environment we have ever seen?

This book is about what makes this kind of leader. For the last 17 years, Common Purpose has been a kind of laboratory in which Julia, like some marvelous alchemist, has been instrumental in identifying and helping to inspire all kinds of people whose authority comes from *them*, not just from what they *do*.

Perhaps the image of the alchemist is not so far-fetched. Really excellent leadership does have a magical element. But Julia is far too hard-headed to take refuge in magic. The enormous success of Common Purpose is that it is based on the proven fact that real leaders – however different their personalities, however diverse their backgrounds – who all see the same situation at the same time, will come to recognize how much they have *in common and* how, together, they can start to change things.

In Julia's world, there is not much room for ideology as an end in itself. Her ideal leaders, like her, are pragmatic, able to forge alliances, good at creating and operating networks. Because their authority comes in part from their personality, they don't feel the need obviously to dominate; they are not at all bad at leading from behind. Anyone who has seen Julia at work will have seen the elliptical way in which she works as a leader and how often the conclusion is the one she wanted right at the start.

I recall one meeting, chaired by Julia, which I was convinced was going to go nowhere. And yet a very disparate group of people arrived at the same conclusion almost without realizing who had got them there.

Years ago, this was sometimes called "natural" authority. Julia has it in abundance and knows it is a skill that is more in demand than ever, and it is one that can be taught and refined, as she shows in this book. Perhaps it is not entirely a coincidence that Common Purpose's success has coincided with what is sometimes called the end of ideology. The old "oughts," the old "isms" made a certain, directive leadership style much easier.

Now the battle lines are anything but clear. Alliances form around issues and then re-form around others. The distinction between private and public sector, for example, is now blurred in almost every area, from health care to prisons, in ways which would have seemed inconceivable 20 years ago.

Julia saw early on that these lines were blurring, and Common Purpose is magnificent testimony to her prescience. Like her, these new kinds of leader refuse to accept that they should stay "in their box," stick to what they know. 2009 is the 200th anniversary of the birth of Charles Darwin, one of the greatest thinkers of all time. The striking thing about him was that he did not recognize boundaries; he just went where his research took him. The result was an amazing, integrated whole even though, by today's standards, he had none of the "qualifications" which are now thought to be a prerequisite for authority. Julia's leaders also have this confidence, the authority to go where the issue takes them.

I have worked with Julia for a lot of the 17 years that she has "been" Common Purpose. During that time many thousands of people have been on its programs. They can't all be Wilberforce or John Lewis. But you only have to attend a gathering of Common Purpose "graduates" to see that they are not "ordinary" leaders either. Julia is fonder of "citizens" – a word which can sometimes conjure up the Scarlet Pimpernel and all those citizens gathered at the foot of the guillotine. But, for her, citizenship by itself implies very clear and very important leadership responsibilities. Or to paraphrase Robert Kennedy: there are those who ask why and then there are those who ask why not? There is no greater tribute than to say that Julia, magnificently, is one of the latter.

Sir David Bell
Chair, *The Financial Times*

Thank you

Thank you to the many colleagues and friends in many countries who have given me their time, ideas, and words for this book. Very few of the ideas are just mine; they are all gleaned from many conversations over the last year as I have become more and more fascinated by the subject. Two people could only give me their time and ideas: they both run huge companies, and did not want me to quote them directly. So I have called them "Stranger One" and "Stranger Two," because I don't want to steal their ideas without giving them credit. They provide crucial pieces in the jigsaw of leading beyond authority.

Above all, thank you to Richard Warren, who has spent many hours putting my ideas in order and helping me get them out of my head and on to paper.

Julia Middleton

Introduction

We all know about leadership. You take on a task, with a budget and a team. You're the one in authority, you're in charge. You set the objectives and have a timescale. And then it's your job to pull it all together, to motivate the people who work for you and get on with delivering it.

On the whole, most leadership development tells us how to perform well in this situation. But, increasingly, this is not the only sort of leadership we are being called to deliver on. Often, you're not in charge: in fact, no one is. There is no budget. And there are no people who have to work for you.

Executives have to produce change within their organizations but across functions they don't control. Policemen have to work alongside health and housing professionals. Politicians have to draw together communities to plan for the future. Directors have to work with partners outside their business. Non-executives have to influence decisions that are not theirs to make.

Across every sector, this is happening more and more. Boundaries are blurring. Authority is becoming less clear-cut. Partnership is proliferating. The traditional leadership tools work – but nothing like as well, or as often, as they used to.

Increasingly, you need to supplement them with others. That's what this book is about.

PART 1

What is leading beyond authority?

Was there ever a time when (to paraphrase John Donne) leaders could operate as islands, entire of themselves? Frankly, I doubt it. But if there was, that time has gone. Many organizations operate in silos: with each division or department looking upwards and so seldom sideways at issues that cross the verticals. They need leaders who can see across the whole organization and make the sum of the parts greater than the whole. They need leaders who understand the value of networks which extend far beyond the traditional confines – and, more importantly, know how to lead them. The opportunities (and threats) ahead will not come neatly parceled to fit the department, or division, or sector, or culture, or even country into which we have arranged ourselves. They will cross boundaries and come through walls – and our leaders need to be able to do this too.

And it doesn't stop at organizations. Society needs leaders who can overcome the silo problem inside their organization – and then move across different spheres of activity outside it and connect them too. Then, perhaps, we can start to shift the "silo problem" in society as well.

This requires leaders who are prepared to challenge the "butt out" culture that tells everyone to "stick to their knitting" and stop interfering where they don't belong. Leaders who can take responsibility for problems other than their own, both within organizations and in society at large. Leaders who can still lead when their legitimacy is constantly in question.

We need to nurture these leaders. We need to give them the confidence they need to legitimize themselves and challenge the old ways. And we need to make them successful as they create new ones. Why do so many leaders in this situation withdraw to their home territory, bruised, muttering about "them" as they retreat? Because they simply do not know how to lead people who are not "theirs." They do not know how to adapt when the instincts that led them to success in their own field do not work outside it.

I call this "leading beyond authority." It's not about having authority but choosing not to use it; it's about having no authority at all (and sometimes less than that). It's about *earning* legitimacy with ideas that resonate – and an approach to leadership that means people end up willingly granting authority to you.

This is vital. For organizations, for the people who lead them, for the people they lead, and for society as a whole. And it's different from conventional leadership: not completely different, but different enough to be worth exploring. And, for leaders of all kinds, in all kinds of positions and organizations, I think it is worth learning how to do. Or, at the very least, learning how to do better.

The circle of authority

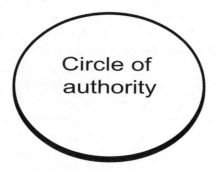

Most leaders have an inner circle, where they are in authority. Of course, they must motivate their people in it but, ultimately, they can bonus or sack them. The leaders have authority; they are "in control"; they can choose to use their authority to a greater or lesser extent, but everyone knows that this is the bottom line. On the whole, the people they lead are minded to follow, even if they won't give it their all unless they are motivated and inspired by their leader. I call this the "circle of authority." Its boundaries are usually coterminous with the leaders' budget. It is often a department or a division or a section of the organization they operate in. They have usually been appointed or elected to the role. Sometimes it's huge, sometimes it's small, but everyone knows what it is – and where it ends. Most of the recognition leaders get is for what they achieve in this space; and most of the leadership development they receive as they progress (under the heading of supervisory training, or management development, or leadership education) aims to make them more effective in this circle.

The first outer circle

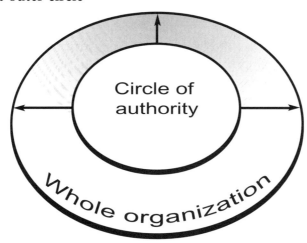

Then there is a first outer circle. This represents the whole organization within which the leader operates. At any given time, there is a very good chance that the chief executive will be trying to get all the leaders, at every level, in all the different core circles, to operate beyond them – for the benefit of the organization as a whole. Alan Lafley, who runs Procter & Gamble, apparently says: "*A measure of a person's power is that their circle of influence is greater than their circle of control.*" Indeed, there is almost no chief executive in the world, be it of a company (big or small), a hospital, a civil service, whatever the entity, who does not want to get their organization operating horizontally as well as vertically (just as long as it is both – and not one at the expense of the other). They want the parts operating cleverly together so that they maximize the effectiveness of the whole. They want two and two to make eight.

Many organizations wrestle with the silo problem. Banks, where great risks have not been spotted. New technology companies, where constant invention and reinvention is crucial. Manufacturers, where any waste needs eradicating. Service providers, where the customer can rapidly be lost through lack of connectivity. Or in the public sector, where the many services all interconnect.

Unwelcome interference

So the chief executives try to change the culture. They change the structure. Even, in some brave cases, they change the way they analyze the performance indicators. (I'm told that one of the biggest investment banks in the City of London became so convinced of the need for change that they seriously considered no longer analyzing profitability *at all* so as to break the vertical structures that had built up around geography and lines of business.) In very rare cases, they restructure the rewards systems to encourage people to take wider responsibility. Because they know that it's in this outer ring that their best people add the most value to the organization.

But when leaders who have been persuaded to venture into the first outer circle actually do it, they find a very different world. Where there is *no* authority. And their legitimacy is constantly in question, with other leaders demanding to know why they are messing about in territory that is not their own.

When I speak about leading beyond authority, it's fun to tease the audience. When I first mention the expression, their eyes glaze over and I know they are thinking "busybodies." So I catch them – as they glaze over – and say: "*This is the problem. Your instinctive response. Thinking 'busybodies,' rather than leaders who are prepared to look beyond their budget and see the bigger picture. You illustrated the challenge beautifully the moment you all glazed over.*" And it is indeed this response that never fails to put people off trying to work outside their core circles. After all, no one wants to be a busybody, to appear so arrogant as to assume authority before they have been given it. However, we need more leaders who will run the gauntlet of criticism about their legitimacy and take on problems other than their own. Because, as a senior civil servant said to me recently: "*It's ridiculous, indeed almost the highest form of arrogance, to assume that all the problems will fit neatly into the departments we have organized ourselves into.*" I would argue that we won't just fail to solve the problems. We'll miss opportunities too.

Coalitions and long games

There's another problem in the first outer circle. Not only is your legitimacy questioned in a way that you have never dreamed of (and certainly never had to face in your circle of authority), but it can be horrible out there. It takes forever to make anything happen. The time scales are ridiculous. And you have to spend your whole time building coalitions if you want to get anything done. To many, the temptation to revert back into the core circle of authority is huge. Of course, deep inside, you also know that it's your achievements in this inner circle that will really gain you recognition. Sir Derek Higgs is Chair of Alliance and Leicester plc and chaired the Independent Review of Non-Executive Directors. He says: *There are centripetal forces in human nature. People look inwards rather than outwards and the further you go out, the harder it gets. Leadership development needs to seriously invest in taking people off the tramlines and out of their comfort zone."*

I talked about this with a very bright director of a successful Internet-based company. He had shared an idea with the American CEO, who then invited him to the States to test it out. It was a classic "leading beyond authority" opportunity – and he found the experience extremely frustrating: *"It takes too long, it's too complex, with multiple stakeholders, many out to neutralize you, none in a position to just say 'yes.' It's better to focus on my own area, where what I achieve will be recognized. And it's not as if I don't have enough to do already. Never again."*

He saw it as horrible. I'd say it's different.

The second outer circle

The second outer circle represents society as a whole. There are many reasons – some organizational, some societal – for leaders to operate in this space.

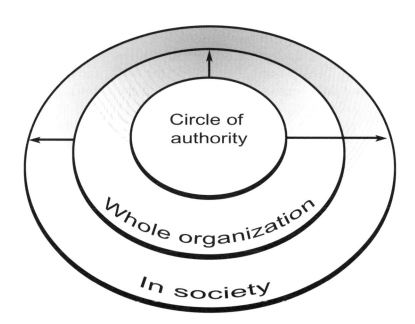

License to operate

Most organizations now acknowledge that their license to operate is not a given: they need to connect with, and convince, the outside world. They have shareholders and partners to keep onside. The boundaries between the organization, its stakeholders, and the outside world are becoming more fluid. Contracting out has become more common. Corporate social responsibility is speeding ever higher up the agenda. The organization's leaders know that operating in isolation is not an option – and that many things that happen in the outer circle have a direct impact on their ability to operate.

In some cases, it goes even further. They know that, however excellent their organization becomes, if other organizations are not going in the same direction, none of them will succeed. So organizations need their leaders to connect with the outside world. Maybe now the skills of leading a network are going to become as important as those of leading an organization. Sure, the leaders can send out ambassadors to do the connecting for them: marketing professionals, corporate social responsibility experts, policy developers. But sometimes the ambassador is not enough – and the leaders have to do it themselves. If the message is to be got across and the outside world is to be reconciled with yours, the communication has to be direct. In any case, if the leaders don't get out into the changing world, they run the risk of not being sufficiently connected to spot the opportunities and threats there. And they sure won't know how to grab them – or duck them – when they come. They run the risk of developing "group think," and becoming convinced that theirs is the best and only way of doing things. And they won't spot talent in unfamiliar places.

Civil society needs leaders

The outer circle needs these leaders. Not simply as representatives of organizations that need to connect with the outside world, but as individual citizens in their own right. We all live in society – and society needs the brains and abilities of all of us if it is to run well. Democracy is not just about voting every few years and then whingeing in the intervening period about politicians not being able to run the place properly. We all need to engage as citizens. Some will do it by entering politics. Others will do it by standing up as leaders of civil society. But we all need to be involved.

And many leaders need civil society

A lot of leaders aren't just out there because it's useful to them as professionals, or because society needs them. They are there because they want to be. They want to make a difference beyond their core circle – and civil society is what enables them to do it. As I watch people on Common Purpose programs, in Teesside in the north of England, or in Dublin, or Johannesburg, or Frankfurt, I see a re-emergence of philanthropy. And a growing belief that politicians cannot – and cannot be expected to – address society's issues on their own. As citizens, this new generation of leaders is more likely to volunteer. They worry about short-termism and about the cultural fragmentation that they see going on around them. It's the silo problem again: but across society – and writ in very large letters. For me, the best illustration of this came from the program in Birmingham. A young participant described feeling as if she had been in a maze, where every organization and each community has its own separate section, until finally someone cut down the hedges for her. Now she could survey the whole landscape. She could spot short cuts – and avoid dead ends. But perhaps mostly this new generation worries that, if leaders do not address these issues head on, trust in both leaders and the very idea of leadership will erode.

Prepare for tough questions

If leaders, having braved the first outer circle, come out to the next one, they are in for an even bigger surprise. If they found the questions about their legitimacy hard to handle in the first outer circle, the interrogation out here is of a whole new order. Now they are told – loudly and publicly – to butt out. They are hit with a barrage of legitimacy questions. Most of which start with "by what right…?" or "on whose authority…?" I well remember going to meet the leader of Manchester City Council about three years after I had started Common Purpose. As I walked in, he welcomed me with: *"I wouldn't have let you into my office two years ago."* He explained that, when he had been elected leader of the city two years before, he was determined that, through his own civil leadership, he would produce huge change. And he had. Manchester was on a roll, a big roll. You could feel it wherever you went. But now he recognized that, to go further, he needed others. That he would need all leaders of civil society, all over Manchester, to help. That he could not do it alone. So he had decided that maybe Common Purpose could be useful if we could find, inspire, connect, and develop more leaders. Especially the next generation of leaders in Manchester.

The great "they"

Both in organizations and in society, we have become far too good at delegating everything to the great "they." This can be politicians. Or "the people upstairs." Or "the experts." Sometimes, it's just someone – anyone – else. What we don't realize is that, sometimes, there is no "they." It's "us." Or even "me." It has almost gone so far that, when you do stand up, you are seen as acting illegitimately, unless you are a politician, the boss, or a professional carrying the relevant institutional or departmental brief. Jude Kelly is Artistic Director at the South Bank Centre in London. She says: "*We cannot wait to be given legitimacy. We need to legitimize ourselves.*"

Bigger coalitions and even longer long-games

And that's not all. If time scales in the first outer circle were long, they are even longer out here – and the coalitions you need to build are even bigger. The centripetal force becomes even more compelling. Go back to Derek Higgs: "*The further out you get, the harder it gets.*"

It's not for everyone. But ...

So it gets tougher, the further out you go. Lots of very successful, talented people don't want to go out there, or don't see the point. They add real value to their organizations and to society by doing what they do well. And that's fine, as long as they don't sit on the sidelines throwing rocks at the growing number of leaders who do want to move out beyond their authority. This book is intended for the ones who do want to go further. What can they learn from people who have already done it? What do they need to learn (or unlearn) to make the transition successfully? And how do they avoid retreating with a bitter "never again"? Or worse, with the stubborn conviction that change in the outer circles simply isn't possible, so it's not worth trying?

Step by step or leaps and bounds?

Do you need to progress circle by circle? In some ways, that helps, so that you take sensible steps outwards. Don't do it in one big bound. Julia Cleverdon, Chief Executive of Business in the Community, says: "*Do it in small incremental steps.*" Circle by circle.

This brings to mind a conversation with Dame Gill Morgan, who is Chief Executive of the NHS Federation. She is concerned about the challenges in the health sector for people who make the leap in one go – from local doctor to the non-executive chair of a Health Trust, for example – and are thrown very much into the deep end of leadership. I think the steps need to be incremental – but they must not be too cautious. They just need to be well judged.

Sometimes jumping a stage is welcome. I have a friend who was UK Chairman of a huge global company. While still there, he also became Chair of an international charity. He talks of the relief when he leapt right out to the very outer "society" circle. He had spent so much time and effort leading beyond authority within the huge and complex organization he knew and loved that he had become exhausted by it. When he moved to the outer circle, he was expecting worse and, for him, it was a huge relief.

On the whole, though, it's worth going circle by circle. James Ramsbotham is Chief Executive of the North East Chamber of Commerce. He agrees that there is value in moving carefully and accumulating learning as you go. But he makes a very important point about the progression and what it does for the leaders who do it successfully: "*As you keep going out of your core circle, and you get better at it, your circles expand too. As you progress within your organization, your core circle gets bigger, often because you have got better at negotiating your way around the other circles.*"

Success across the circles

Beware: success in one circle does not *guarantee* success in the others. Over the years, I have worked with some amazing campaigners who are hugely successful on the outer rim of the outer circle. They take their time, they create their own legitimacy, they build glorious coalitions, and much more. But, back at base, within their authority, their core circle, it's a shambles. They aren't even prepared to delegate. I have also worked with fantastic chief executives who are hugely successful in their core circle and then fail miserably (and, to them, very unexpectedly) in the outer circles.

Can you bring back what you learn out there?

Definitely. I believe that people who learn to lead beyond their authority will find it useful when they return to their core circle. Because they will go just that little bit further before exercising their authority within the organization – and the people they lead may well find this exciting. It will also prepare them for a shock which every single chief executive I have ever spoken to describes: that the higher you go in an organization and the closer you get to achieving authority, the more illusory it becomes. In reality, the moments when people with authority can really use it become fewer and further between. Leading beyond authority is good preparation for this revelation.

Full circle

Sometimes, when you go into the outer circles, a strange thing happens. Leaders who have learned to do without authority are given it. Volunteered it by the people they are leading.

Willingly and naturally. Because they have earned it.

There are people who say that the real test of a leader is whether he or she can lead without authority. It sounds good – but I am not sure that it is true. I think the best leaders can lead when they have authority and when they don't. The point is that they don't *need* authority to be able to do it. The best can do it all. And there are plenty of them. They are not successful all the time – but no one ever is. The trouble is that most of them don't think about how they do it. They say to me: *"But doesn't everyone do it like this?"*

If only.

SCENARIO: WHEN DID YOU START MOVING ACROSS THE CIRCLES – AND WHY?

Lord Puttnam, President of UNICEF (UK) and Advisor to the Department of Education. Prior to that, a film-maker.

Hubris was the first reason. I had just won the Palme D'Or in Cannes and there was nowhere else to go. I knew I could not become one of those people who looks back sometime in the future and says "I could have done more."

There were then two factors that moved me on to the outer circle. One was to do with timing. I was asked at the right time. If Labour had won the '92 election, it would have been wrong. But, in '97, the timing was right. I was ready to try new things.

The other was that I heard myself say "Yes" on the phone one night when I was asked. It was about as planned as that!

Thinking back though, I don't think I would have gone into the outer circles if I had not been confident that I was wanted for all my skills and abilities. It was not just about the success or knowledge I had acquired in my core circle, my ability to make movies. I wanted to really move out and not get sucked back into the film industry.

Whichever circle I am in, I always prefer the cafe style. I love the small teams and the discussions. All I really need is a pen, some paper, and a phone.

James Ramsbotham is Chief Executive of the North East Chamber of Commerce and former Chair of Esh Group. Prior to that, he was at Barclays Bank and, before that, a Captain in the Army.

I am not sure that I have ever stayed within any boundaries. I was always that child who was fascinated with everyone and wanted to learn everything I could, whether it was from the school bus driver or the Secretary of State for Industry, who came to give a lecture at our school. I wanted to know everything I could. It was the way I was "brought up."

When I joined the Army, it was the same. In Northern Ireland, I would seek out all sorts of unlikely people to meet and talk to, particularly if they had a completely different point of view. Members of IRA families. Political leaders. Even members of the Garda. I am interested in every point of view – and I know how easy it is to cloud one's judgment by having too strong an opinion of one's own.

I remember, in a counter-terrorist situation, my police colleagues encountered a traffic management problem which they could not solve. I asked our driver, who had been listening in silence, what he thought. He had the answer straight away but was amazed that I had asked him for his opinion. The police were even more stunned.

I never missed an opportunity, not just to go out of my circle, but also to go places within my circle that others did not go. For example, as an officer, I went out on patrol in Northern Ireland as a rifleman (most of the others had no idea who I was). I was not alone in such activity – it was the norm in my regiment. Deliberate attempts to engage with a wider circle were not frowned upon, as they are in some regiments – and in the US army, which encourages you to stay within the confines of the base. We would have gone mental if we had just done that.

Banking was the perfect next opportunity for me. It required me to meet business people of every shape and size, take an active interest in their affairs and, as I quickly found, introduce people to each other and widen *their* circles in so doing. My desire to challenge and see things from other points of view gave me several opportunities to challenge accepted practices in Barclays. Eventually, I was asked to restructure the way in which we did banking in Newcastle and this was then adopted throughout the country. It meant engaging with influencers who had been previously ignored. In my final role at Barclays – in marketing – I was always outside the core circle. Then again, marketers should be out there all the time anyway.

I have often done things merely because they were fun. The day job has not always offered sufficient stimulus. A medium-sized construction company is a fairly conservative place. The fact that we were widely recognized for our work in the community is testament to what can be achieved by pushing the boundaries out. We twinned with a failing local school and played a part in its transformation. We successfully employed ex-offenders and ex-addicts, and played our part in rehabilitation. None of these directly related to the day job, but all were about benefitting the community.

Pete Connolly is Chief Executive of Yorkshire Design.

I left my core circle because I got so angry. Because I love Leeds and I don't think there are enough voices in the city who ask difficult questions of those in power.

So I started asking them. Speaking up at events, writing letters to the editor about all kinds of issues. I did that for a while, but then I realized that the local newspaper was using me – they would regularly phone me for comments. I was always quoted, and as negatively as possible. So I went back into purdah, into my own circle for a while.

Then a group of us realized that we were leaving the difficult questions to be asked by all the bodies that in theory should be doing it, but can't. Because they have got sucked into the system, they have become neutered and they can't criticize because they have become part of things. Surely, we asked ourselves, there must be some way to be collective without being political? So we started the FU Club. When you apply for planning permission in the city, you get a letter back with a reference code that always starts with the letters "FU" followed by some numbers. We think that's how our local government feels about citizens in Leeds.

Richard Greenhalgh is Chair of First Milk Limited and Templeton College, Oxford, and former Chair of Unilever in the UK.

I came to the outer circles quite late in my career – and, at first, very much as an ambassador for the company.

In the late 1990s, genetically modified organisms were entering the soya market and my company initially decided to accept this modified crop. Technically, it behaved no differently than unmodified soya. However, some interest groups, Greenpeace and the Soil Association in particular, objected strongly. There was no advantage to consumers in GMO soya but, for one of our products with significant organic and vegetarian consumers, GMO soya was highly suspect. Sales fell. Appointed as UK Chairman that year, I initially led with a rational approach, aiming to convince consumers it was no less safe than non-modified soya and articulating a future where GMO products would actually improve quality and even enhance health (e.g. in tomatoes). We partnered with other companies in this, and defended the food industry in general and the company reputation in particular.

It didn't work. The company was being attacked in the media ("Frankenstein foods") and the retailers started to change their position from GMO support to rejection or choice. I moved to the organizational circle, working with outsiders: involving the government, briefing the media and starting a dialogue with Greenpeace, the Soil Association, and other NGOs. But it was too late. Rehearsing answers for the TV with an ex-*Sun* reporter, I struggled. The pro-GMO case was difficult to make. So we thought again.

We held focus groups externally and reviewed our position internally. I talked to friends. They were largely unsympathetic to genetic modification. Focus groups supported it for life saving and even life-enhancing purposes, but not for food. The company in the UK reverted to non-GM crops. We failed to see the warning signs until it was too late. Had I realized three years earlier, I would have tested the societal circle first. Had it been more positive at this stage, I would have set out to take the media and the NGOs with us. Finally, I would have organized ourselves better internally and led the change.

It was an excellent learning process for a leader! I then became more and more interested in the outer circles. I have since taken roles that have continued to push my thinking outwards.

Cyril Ramaphosa is Chair of the Constitutional Assembly of South Africa.

When I started on the task of sorting out the mine workers, I consciously chose to leave the authority I had. Because I took the view that others before me had failed by trying to operate it this way and that I would be better off taking on the task with no authority at all.

In the 1970s, the trade union movement began to surge. In those days there was an unquestioned principle that you never went to the bosses. I broke it – and went to ask permission to organize the workers. Asking the bosses for permission was like going to Alcatraz and asking for permission to organize a prison break-out.

I knew I was taking a big risk. Many before me had tried to organize the mine workers; there had been many such attempts between 1946 and 1982. I knew I had to do something new. Why would I take a long detour (which is what it was) and break a fundamental principle about working with the bosses? I attracted a lot of criticism from the trade unions and the ANC. It was a painful and lonely path to take.

But I knew that the authority I appeared to have was the wrong one. The miners were living in an almost military environment – they were like hostages. I knew that I needed to move outside the rules, outside the traditional way of organizing the workers, and outside the authority that I had been given.

So I went to the Chamber of Mines and asked for permission to operate in the mines: for offices and resources and food for my officials. The timing was right because a report had just come out saying that black miners needed to organize into legalized trade unions.

Once we got going properly, the workers stopped feeling so browbeaten – and stopped behaving like hostages. It was like lancing a boil: there was an out-flowing of this quest for freedom – and we became the fastest growing union in the world, with 360,000 members eventually.

So I eventually moved back into authority – but a different one. To get there, I had to make a detour and operate way beyond my authority first. If I had not taken that detour and moved way outside my authority, it would have not been possible to organize the mine workers so quickly. Of course, the strikes they then backed played a crucial part in making the country ungovernable and causing the breakdown of the apartheid government. The detour was all part of achieving our original objective.

PART 2

So why do it?

The case against going into the outer circles is compelling. It has to be, given the number of leaders who choose not to do it. They prefer to stay in the space where they have worked hard to build their reputation and where they are credible and respected. Maybe they want to enjoy their success. In any case, people who have done it before will tell them that many of the instincts that they have developed within their authority – that they know work and that have become intuitive to them – will become counter-intuitive in the outer two circles. In fact, sometimes they produce the opposite effect. Moving to the outer circles would mean proving themselves all over again. It might not take as long this time, but they will have to do it. Because it's different. Indeed, as Ned Sullivan, Chairman of the Greencore Group in Ireland, says: *"Not all leaders can do it. Success in the core does not guarantee you will be effective in the outer rims. In fact, not that many are."*

Few rewards

The rewards certainly won't be financial – and maybe won't be in reputation either. Pam Chesters used to work at BP and is now well ensconced in the outer rim of the outer circle as non-executive Chair of both the Royal Free Hospital Trust and English Churches Housing Group. She finds it hard sometimes to recruit new board members for her huge hospital based in north London: *"The NHS is not exactly a comfortable place to be at the moment. There is a considerable amount of grief relative to the change you can produce. Reputations are being damaged, and not always fairly. It's not that people are looking for external recognition, but you do have to feel within yourself that you are able to make a difference, otherwise what's the point?"*

Julie Baddeley is a non-executive director of Greggs plc. She says the same: *" If you spend almost all of your time in the outer circles as I do, then the real issue is how do you give yourself a sense of achieve-*

ment? You never get to say to yourself: I warned them about this, or suggested that, and they acted and as a result the business is better. It's hard to see where you have made a difference."

Over the last two years, Vince McGinlay has had a leading beyond-authority role as Director of Supply Chain at Marks & Spencer, the troubled UK retailer that is starting to turn the corner and come back to what it was. His task was to sort out problems in his division, which meant crossing over just about every other function in the business: *"It was not that anyone saw me as a threat: they were happy to leave things that crossed boundaries to me and they weren't just dumping stuff either. It was the misery of endlessly running after agreement. You needed the three Ps – Patience, Pragmatism, and Persistence – in bucket loads."* He adds that you don't want *everyone* in an organization leading beyond their authority. It would be like watching kids play football: *"They all chase after the ball every time it's kicked. It's only as they get older that they realize they have to learn to play in position, and that, if you are the goalkeeper, you are unlikely to score many goals."*

Reason 1: good business

Good chief executives are determined to make their operations perform to maximum effect. They are convinced that the silo approach eventually does damage. And they know that the organization needs to connect with the outside world. So they lead from the front – and lead beyond their authority themselves. They operate across the circles and connect the organization with society, and they expect their people to do the same. In so doing, they extend their radar, spot new ideas, develop trust between their own and other organizations, make alliances, and discover trends they need to watch. It's simply good business. As James Ramsbotham warns: *"If you don't, you tend to get more and more shut out. You make assumptions without even knowing you have made them. And you are narrowing your world, without even knowing you are doing it."*

Sir David Varney is Chair of HM Revenue & Customs and former Chair of O$_2$. Prior to that, he was Chief Executive of Shell and then British Gas. He says the same: *"If you are not in the outer circle, you can miss the trends. Or you spot them late, by which time you can't do anything about their tidal wave effect. You have to spot them in that window when the concern was growing. Why did McDonald's not spot that what was a fantastic success was going to become a major contributor to obesity? Is Tesco spotting that people are beginning to question their power now? Why didn't the car industry see that, far from being the source of mobility, they were soon going to be seen as the source of pollution? Leaders have to be in the outer circles, spotting these social forces, hearing even the small voices. Let's face it, there are not a lot of Falstaffs out there 'talking truth unto power': so you have to be out there yourself, listening very, very hard."*

This is not just about the leaders at the top. It's about middle managers too. Many ask for more leadership development – but don't understand that the next step is not upwards, but outwards. They have to start leading beyond their own team, plant, department, division. They will have to start leading outwards, however uncomfortable it feels, before they can go upwards. They have to understand that they have a responsibility to their team to influence not only upwards but outwards too. That, however good they are with their own team, they are betraying them if they don't do this. It's nothing to do with personal aggrandizement – it's about their duty as leaders. Maybe they would rather not have to try to attempt to influence the IT strategy – but they have to. They cannot just sit back and receive it, or put up with it. There are decisions made in the rest of the business that will have a direct impact on their people: so they have to influence them, whether they have the authority to do it or not.

Reason 2: fresh territory

Some leaders move outwards because, for whatever reason, they haven't fully succeeded inside their circle of authority (or couldn't succeed), so they want a broader canvas. This is, sadly, not uncommon: and it means that there are some people in the outer circle who are not particularly successful there either. However, there are people in the outer circles who are almost liberated as they get out of authority – and become huge achievers in the new context. Just as success in the core circle does not guarantee success in the outer circles, so people who have not starred in the core circle can become hugely effective in the outer ones. For some leaders, as Tom Frawley, Ombudsman for Northern Ireland, says: *"Power and authority can become a prison. You are forced, quite rightly, to fight for your organization. And you are constricted by the demands, very appropriately, that you be accountable."* Being set free, for some, can be glorious.

Reason 3: the "quarter-life crisis"

For others, it's not that they haven't succeeded – but that they haven't done it *yet*. They want another arena to develop in while they prove themselves in their core circle. In 2004 Common Purpose did a survey of younger leaders, because we were developing programs to meet their needs and we wanted to understand them more. In their late twenties, they talked of a "quarter-life crisis." They described the difficulty of being told to concentrate and keep their heads down until they proved themselves in their core circle. They talked of having to pack away all their interest in the wider world and how frustrating that is, because they wanted a balance of their core and the outer circles so they could make an impact both within the organization and in society. It was clear that this was a big contributor to many of them leaving their first and second jobs.

Recently, I spoke to a young colleague in Glasgow, Louise Nolan, about what she gets from being on the board of a housing association. She is in her early twenties (probably she brings down the average age of the board by ten years). She works on the board because she has lived in the area, in rented accommodation of various kinds – "*with varying degrees of dodgy heating systems and nailed-down windows*" – for years. And because change is on its way for this part of Glasgow, with huge amounts of money being pumped in, and she wants to be part of it. First, she described what they got from having her: "*a voice of reason in ASBO-mania debates*" (ASBOs, "Anti Social Behaviour Orders," are used to control the behavior of neighbors, particularly unruly teenagers). On behalf of the board, she attends meetings on the estate with young people: "*Last week, I met a group to discuss CCTV surveillance, which is all over the city. They were all shocked to discover that many of the cameras are not for police use but were bought by Housing Associations, which could use the footage to prove breaches of tenancy, leading ultimately to evictions. We were all struck by the power of the Housing Association over people's lives. One stunned 15-year-old realized that what she saw as naughty drinking with her friends could mean that she and her family could become homeless. For me, [the biggest shock] was the realization that I was part of the leadership of the organization that had this power.*" Louise says that she is learning to use her influence within the board, and with other decision-makers within the city. It is getting her to operate "*outside her usual haunts.*" In my view, it is also developing her leadership skills in ways no employer – even Common Purpose – could.

Reason 4: it's stifling in here ...

James Ramsbotham never allowed himself a quarter-life crisis. He has been very successful, in the Army, at Barclays Bank and in the northeast of England. In each core role, he has also taken on others in the outer circle, because: *"You get bored with the core circle and with the people there who are too focused. Of course, we need them to be focused, because it's the secret of their success, but it does not suit all of us. I find the core circle stifling. You do it because you need the money flowing in but, for me, it's not enough."*

This raises another important point. There are people who are at their best in the core circle. And they are valuable there. There are also times when the most far-sighted leader has to concentrate the vision inwards and not outwards. It will probably be when the organization is in trouble and is struggling to make two and two produce four, never mind eight. Then the organization may decide to forego the benefits of its best people operating beyond their authority, and ask them to concentrate their efforts uninterrupted in their core areas. But such times pass. And, when they do, the organization will need its leaders to add value outside the core circle again.

Reason 5: specialism can be stifling too

There are those who find their specialism constraining, particularly if it is going to be hard to prove their success in their core circle as a result. Though told they are crucial, promising, exciting, and impressive, they know they are not in the right part of the business to be able to prove themselves. Amy Fawcett is Vice Chair at Morgan Stanley International. She realized that, as a lawyer (and therefore not in the revenue side of the business), it was going to be very hard to make her mark, so she began to move outwards at an early stage in her career. As she says: *"Sometimes, success in the outer circles gives you enhanced credibility in the inner one. You become more interesting, more networked, better at reading a room, and, because you're dealing with such a wide variety of people, better at building coalitions. To an extent, you develop a bit of a reputation and increased credibility. Colleagues start to think you can have a similar impact internally, with the business, with clients."*

I remember a dinner to explain Common Purpose to the new HR director of a huge accountancy firm that puts people on our programs. The first Common Purpose participant from the firm to speak was a specialist in a particularly arcane corner of tax legislation. He said that he had loved the program, but that it had brought no direct benefit to the business. All he had acquired was "chitchat." My heart sank – no more applications from here, then. Immediately, one of his colleagues slipped in: *"John, you do know, that, prior to going on Common Purpose, none of us would let you meet a client?"*

Reason 6: personal development

A lot of leaders are determined to develop themselves personally. To push out their own boundaries. To switch up the bandwidth on their radar screens and make sure they put themselves into new positions that will require them to think differently and take risks. I call this the "hourglass effect." You start your career broad and, as you progress, you become more and more knowledgeable in a smaller and smaller field. Then you get to the big next job that is going to require you to be broad again, so that you can make the alliances, crossing and connecting the circles – and nothing seems to have prepared you for it. As David Varney says: *"Most of us are developed to be followers, agents of organizations. We are encouraged to stick to our core circle and to try to keep away from the boundaries. At the most, we go into boundary management, watching the outside world from in here and trying to analyze it. Then, suddenly, we get appointed to the top job and have to deal with the outside world."*

Organizations talk about needing to rekindle an entrepreneurial spirit amongst their people. In my view, by far the best way to do this is to go into new areas. To challenge what might have become "group think" in your own circle. To learn to adapt, survive (and even thrive) in the outer circle – the more unfamiliar the territory, the better. Back to David Varney: *"You need leaders with an appetite to learn. The Fortune 500 list is very dynamic, with many companies dropping out and a few surviving longer term. The average life of a company is 40 years (and decreasing). The survivors tend to be successful organizations because of their capacity to adapt and learn. The failures tend to be companies whose leadership lacked the huge appetite to learn."*

Reason 7: to test yourself

There is an endless nagging question in many leaders' minds: *"Am I up to it?"* I first met Tarek Ben Halim when he was an investment banker at Goldman Sachs. A few months later, he left Goldman and took on a variety of new roles, one of which was to start the Arab Learning Initiative (which would support and grow social enterprises in Egypt and eventually in many other Arab countries). It cost him time and money – and it was a big risk calling in so many favors. So why did he do it? He is quite clear: *"It was the temptation to test myself."*

Diana Parker is Chair of Withers solicitors. She says: *"Let's face it, many leaders don't like it when they are not the boss. They have worked hard to get where they are, and they want to enjoy it. But, for me, one of the key roles of a leader is to push the boundaries out. Leaders have to make people feel uncomfortable. To do this, you have to feel uncomfortable yourself."*

For me, this may be part of the reason why power corrupts. Because, as leaders become increasingly successful in the core circle, they become reluctant to move out of what has become their comfort zone.

Diana goes on: *"This is one reason why I love entrepreneurs – they are always alive to what's going on. You meet some chief executives of large organizations, who have worked their way up, and they are very impressive. But you cannot stop asking yourself, how much better could they be if they had worked outwards as well as upwards?"*

Reason 8: your success depends on other people's

Some leaders move out because they recognize that their circle of control cannot achieve its maximum potential within the current system – that there is a need for wider change. The divisional head of manufacturing might decide that his/her division cannot fully achieve without changes to the way the marketing function is run, so he/she decides to take on an issue that goes way beyond the divisional budget (or authority). A chief executive might decide that the business will not succeed without some change in legislation, and will move to the outer circle to help bring it about. In each case, the leaders move outwards to bring about a change that will enable them to succeed in their own areas. There are good examples of this across all organizations.

Sandy Forrest is now Director at the Council for Healthcare Regulatory Excellence. He crystallized it best for me: *"For many years, I was a police officer, where the need to take on leadership roles applies throughout, not just at senior levels. Often you were leading beyond authority: in essence, getting people who don't work for you to contribute fully to achieving the desired outcome with you. Policing is always just one element in the infrastructure that keeps a community 'safe' or, at least, feeling safe. Most things require partnership activity. Successful achievement of operational goals is dependent, to an extent, on support, harmonization, and synergy with other organizations. Optimum efficiency on the part of your organization can often achieve little if it is not matched or complemented by action on the part of others – in health, housing or education – who are employed by someone else."*

This is a big new challenge in local government too. If the future role of local authorities is no longer to run services but to provide community leadership and to shape the places they serve, local politicians will need to become ever better at leading across communities and organizations over which they have no direct authority. Lucy de Groot is Executive Director of IDeA, the local government improvement agency. She considers that *"Local government has become very effective at adapting to central government priorities and forgotten how to produce local leadership."* In my view, drawing everyone and everything together will take all the leading beyond authority skills that managers can muster.

Reason 9: making partnerships work

In the public sector in the UK, people are constantly being told to do all things in partnership. Over the last few years, we have developed partnerships for just about everything. The idea of course is entirely right, because everything is interconnected.

But, there are some very different organizations – and agendas – to pull together here. All too often, the whole principle of partnerships has become "the sublimation of loathing in the pursuit of funding." Someone throws a group of people together and tells them that, despite years of slagging each other off, they have to start working in partnership. They will certainly be prepared to sublimate their views if there is funding attached to it – but very little real partnership is being generated. The reality is that it takes a lot of effort to get a group of people who mostly stick to (indeed prefer) their own core to work together. They have to learn to lead beyond their authority: and it takes time. Zenna Atkins is Chair of Places for People, the largest housing association in the UK. She has chaired a fair number of partnerships over the years, and says: *"They all look at things from their own core. You have to coax them to come out and look at the issue again from [a new] angle – and to do it together. It takes some time.*

But, when it works, it's wonderful." Margaret Ford is Chair of urban development company English Partnerships. She too is aware of the difficulty of building real partnerships: *"When I first came here, we had too many leaders who had never been encouraged to step outside their circle of authority. We were almost masterminding communities from the middle of our core circle."*

Reason 10: anger

Then there are leaders who just get angry about something that really riles them; they become utterly determined to do something about it (recognizing, perhaps, that they may be in more of a position to produce change than most). Stranger One asked me not to name him. He runs a huge company in the UK and he told me about getting really, really angry and knowing he just had to act: *"I stumbled into it. I decided I had to do something, because it made me so angry. After the London bombings in 2005, I became aware of how many young British Muslims were in prison in the UK, with no prospects of ever getting a job when they came out. It seemed like madness. So we got going on some ideas."* He told me how much he had learnt by getting involved – and how much it had pushed out his boundaries: *"I think that, sometimes, you have to find things that you can do that are bigger than what you do."*

Let's go back to Tarek Ben Halim, who was born in Libya. The second reason for his starting the Arab Learning Initiative was: *"I always cared about the Arab world and felt incensed and frustrated by what was happening there. I wanted to make a difference but I never found anything already in existence that I could plug into. This initiative allowed me to impact in a way that felt correct to me."* Anger – combined with frustration – seems to move many into this space.

Reason 11: strengthening democracy

Then there are people who know that our democracy needs waking up. People who are sick of hearing the deafening silence of the multitude. They worry that citizenship is in danger of going the same way as sport: becoming increasingly a spectator activity, with fewer and fewer actual players. As Bertrand de Jouvenal warned: *"A society of sheep begets a government of wolves."* More recently, a report from MORI (the biggest polling organization in the UK) said: *"It's not apathy we are seeing, it's disengagement."* I believe that, for democracy to work, we need an active civil society. For me, this is about all of us, as citizens, behaving as leaders and performing the role which leaders in civil society play in a democracy: keeping the difficult issues on the agenda, holding the powerful to account, and being prepared to take on new roles in order to produce change.

Reason 12: making a difference

Of course, some people move into the outer circle because they want to make a difference. Maybe it's in their blood. Maybe it's because they were brought up that way. Maybe they simply care about other people and their problems. Roisín McDonough is Chief Executive of the Arts Council of Northern Ireland and has been an activist in many roles over the years. She explains her motivation, saying: *"My faith defines a lot for me: my approach to family, to community, and certainly to leading beyond my authority."* Narayana Murthy is Chair of Infosys Technologies Limited, the now-global IT company based in India. He puts it another way: *"Many people wonder why I wanted to take such a risk, to create, at that time in India, a company in India that would set a new standard of ethics in business. I had a good job, I was married, I had a small child, and I was brought up middle class. It was no easy decision. But all of us are driven by factors that transcend the hygiene factors: money and position. We all want to do something noble and make a difference to the context."*

Amy Fawcett talks not of beliefs, but of *"the cultural environment in which you spend your early years. I am the eldest child of a very active mother and father, independent thinkers who are deeply committed to the community and a philosophy perhaps best summed up by President Kennedy's brother Robert as 'each person can make a difference and everyone must try.' That deep-seated commitment could probably be traced back for many generations, and it certainly has had an influence on me and my approach to the world in which I live and work."* Maybe this is at the core of what motivates many people to move into the outer circles, even though the risks are high and the probability of success (even if you could define it) small.

In Britain, we have reduced the expression "community service" to a punishment handed out in the courts by a judge: *"I sentence you to three months' community service."* But, for many people, it's not a punishment. It's part of how they were brought up. It is their general approach to life. They believe that, if they are leaders at work, they need to act as leaders in society too. As George Bernard Shaw said:

"This is the true joy of life, the being used for a purpose recognized by yourself as a mighty one. The being a force of nature instead of a feverish, selfish little clod of ailments and grievances complaining that the world will not devote itself to making you happy."

That is a fitting way to return to the final reason Tarek Ben Halim gives for starting the Arab Learning Initiative: *"The pleasure of seeing your ideas become a reality."*

There's no shortage of reasons why you should want to lead beyond your authority. Now we need to work out how to make it an easier ride.

SCENARIO: HOW TO BREAK DOWN SILOS

You work for a well-known bank. You have had an idea for a new payment scheme, which the bank thinks has potential. So it has set you up in a unit to develop that idea. You know you are seen as a pet of the chief executive, and that many of your colleagues don't like the idea. How do you proceed?

Sandy Forrest is Director of the Council for Healthcare Regulatory Excellence and a former Assistant Inspector in the police.

Remember the song that Bing Crosby used to sing: "You've got to accentuate the positive/Eliminate the negative/Latch on to the affirmative/Don't mess with Mister In-Between."[1]

In very simplistic terms, to produce change you need a strategy and it has three elements:

- ❑ the *ends* you seek to achieve
- ❑ the *means* available to you to pursue them
- ❑ the *conditions* that can either help or hinder successful completion.

In this case, the ends are clear (you have an idea and you want to make it work). The means are probably also clear (or will become clear as the project develops). What is important are the conditions. There will be positive conditions that will facilitate the development, and these should be encouraged. There are also negative conditions, and these have to be "turned-around" or neutralized. When you boil it all down, success may well be entirely about managing or neutralizing the negative conditions. These seem to be, firstly, that your colleagues don't like the idea; and secondly, there is some jealousy, or resentment, that you are seen as the chief executive's favorite.

To address the latter, you could do or say something that puts you publicly out of favor with the chief executive, thereby debunking the "pet" view. But this could also jeopardize the support you need for your project to succeed. So live with the label – or maybe even market it as a positive – so long as you strive to show people

---

[1]　"Ac-cent-tchu-ate the positive." Words by John Mercer, music by Harold Arlen. © 1944 Harwin Music Co. All rights administered by Warner/Chappell Music Ltd, London W6 8BS. Reproduced by permission.

that the reason you are the favorite is that you are actually quite good. It is an organizational fact that, the better you are, the more freedom you get. In delivering on objectives, it is often this extra freedom that enables you to succeed. It becomes a virtuous circle where you succeed because your past successes allow you a latitude that is denied to others and that is vital for success.

Now, turning to your colleagues who don't like the idea. You have to "consult" them and use the opportunity to answer their misgivings. You do this on the basis that they are not wrong, just misinformed; and when they have had a chance to understand why your idea has merit, then perhaps you can negotiate, if not their support, then at least their lack of opposition. In managing negative conditions, creating non-combatants out of opposing forces is a major success. Engagement with them in an intelligence-gathering and influencing/ negotiating mode should be the prime objective. Don't get going until you have done this.

I think a charm offensive, on a one-to-one basis, is preferable to dazzling them in a group meeting. At the very least, you should be able to get out of them what they see to be all of the downsides to your idea – allowing you to tailor your strategy to address these issues specifically. So there will be no negative factors you are unaware of and have failed to take into account. The engagement process could possibly engender some ownership, particularly if they believe you are taking their reservations seriously and addressing them, not just getting around them.

In this case, eliminating the negative is the key. Accentuating the positive thereafter becomes easy.

Rudi Bogni is a director of Old Mutual plc and Prospect Publishing, and former Global Head of Private Banking at UBS.

It is unlikely that you have just developed the idea through parthenogenesis in the bath. It must have arisen from discussions you had with colleagues, or it was triggered by something that one or more people said.

Are you sure you understood correctly and fully what they were saying? Did you test it or have they been sending you on a wild goose-chase? Have you tried to co-opt them or get them to partner with you?

Why do so many of your colleagues not like it? Are they just protecting vested interests or do they have valid objections?

Now that you've got the management backing and the resources to make it happen, to fear internal competition would be very silly. So you should open up. Draw up the concept, the plan, and the budget. Walk it around informally to anyone who will care to listen. The lower down the corporate pecking order, the more likely it is that they know where the pitfalls are and where the bones are buried. Without them, you are likely to fail or to produce delays and cost over-runs. Get people involved. Success has many fathers. Trust that the boss will know who is directing the orchestra. The less noise you make, the better the music.

Have milestones. Flow-chart and cost everything you do. Don't allow slippages (even if it means sleeping at the office) and don't let either your boss or your colleagues and supporters push you into overselling what you have done or will achieve. Eventually, a bit bruised, you'll get there.

Tim found himself in this very position when he was at NatWest.

Tim Jones is a director of Capital One Bank (Europe) PLC and former Chief Executive of Retail Banking at NatWest Bank (where he led the introduction of a new payment system).

The project went through three distinct phases. The first was characterized by secrecy, excitement, and a sense that this could be very big and should be pursued. At this stage, the dissenters were few, largely because knowledge about the project was tightly restricted to a small number of people who "needed to know" because of their functional expertise. They did not need to have a strong view of the project; they just needed to provide their input (for example, legal or technical), which they willingly did.

The second stage could not have been more different. The project had successfully achieved its internal milestones and a presentation was made to the senior executives of the company. It seemed to go well, but we were asking for millions of pounds when we had just entered the recession of the early 1990s. The line went dead. We heard nothing and nobody wanted to talk about it. I was aware that there were many people against the venture – it was expensive and risky and the timing was bad.

I then moved from the project and took on another job – but agreed with my new boss that I would continue to work quietly on my idea. I worked very hard that year, establishing what the next steps would be to take the project out of its "hibernation" state. This was all about getting endorsements from third parties.

In the final phase, the secrecy disappeared as we made our first public announcements about the existence of the work. There was a fair amount of internal sniping, as this was a high-profile and exciting venture. We insulated the project (and me) from potential trouble by getting all the money to launch sanctioned by the Board in one submission. This was subject to strict scrutiny from a specially constituted sub-committee of the Board, so there was plenty of oversight, but it took the money out of the regular budgetary battleground. I do not think the project would have survived if it had been forced to fight for its money each budget cycle.

The lessons I took from the experience were these:

❑ If you believe in something, you have to pursue it with a passion. You have to put your career at risk, and you have to negotiate in the light of the prevailing reality. If your project is worthwhile and the environment is fundamentally reasonable, you will get a good hearing, as long as you behave professionally and allow others to disagree.

❑ In the end, all decisions in organizations rest with a handful of people. They will be different people for each decision, but there won't be more than three, four, or five folk around whom the decision rests. You have to identify these people, focus on them as individuals, and work out how best to influence them, including whether to seek to bring them "onside" or whether to go round them.

PART 3

So how different is it out there?

It's different. Not completely different, but different enough to be worth thinking about before you set off.

As a chief executive of a UK bank once told me, as he reflected on power and how he coped with it: "*You have to avoid the flattery and the flak. It's when you don't that you make your big mistakes. And flattery causes the worst.*" This is of course true within all the circles. But it's harder in the outer ones, not least because it's unfamiliar territory. Which makes it much trickier to spot what is flattery and, certainly, what is flak.

Not that different really

Moira Wallace is Director General of Crime, Policing and Counter Terrorism at the Home Office. She says she spends her life coaxing people out of their core circle:

"*All of us find leaving our comfort zones hard: we see it almost as leaving the Earth's atmosphere. Perhaps we all need reminding that a move to another sector or subject won't be utterly unrecognizable. Like English campers who pack their tinned food to travel abroad, we need persuading that there is running water out there, yes, and maybe even a Starbucks! Maybe part of leadership development is to get people to do 'foreign travel' at an early age – before they become too rigid – to give them the confidence that they can create new comfort zones.*"

Sir John Rose, Chief Executive of Rolls-Royce, makes a further point about the need to "travel." He says: "*Beware the clever idiot: there are many of them around. They are well-read, poorly traveled, and staggeringly bright – but they can't translate because they don't understand context and they are often not good at influencing or getting things done.*"

Sometimes, running Common Purpose programs, which take people way out of their comfort zones, has felt rather like preparing leaders for foreign travel. Persuading them that it will be different, but that just because it's different, that does not mean it will be bad or wrong. Richard Ellis is Chief Executive of Kettle Foods and Chair of the East of England Development Agency. I remember when he went on the program. He told me afterwards that he had always been pretty dismissive of leadership in the arts world. It seemed to him to be chaotic and lacking in structure and discipline. On the program with him was the chief executive of a local theatre arts company, who invited him to come and have a good look. To start with, all Richard's prejudices were comfortingly confirmed. It was indeed messy and confused and unstructured and hard to establish who was doing what. But then they came to the moment when the curtain went up and he saw it all come together – with a degree of commitment amongst all the staff – whatever their role – that he found totally inspiring. Here, he decided, was something he could take back from this strange world to his own company that would be of enormous value. He is now Chair of the development company for the region and operating a long way out of his core circle.

Somehow, you have to persuade participants that, if they create a Little England "over there" when they travel, they will miss out on everything they came out to learn and watch and savor and enjoy. I think of many leaders I have seen on charitable boards who don't really want to be there. Sure, they have come out from their core circle (and probably willingly). But they think everyone out here is amateur and flaky and they would rather go back – dash back, actually. You have to persuade them to buy a phrase book, at the least. Or, at best, learn a new language so they can find out what is going on – and that maybe some of it has some reason to it. A logic, even if it's strange.

Then again, I think of Ruth Wishart, the gray-haired dynamo of a journalist and broadcaster in Scotland, who has also been in the middle of just about everything that civil society has made happen there: *"Any time you move up in a job, or on to a new thing, you really hope that the team will be inspiring and really know what they're doing; people who can see and interpret the bigger picture. If they turn out not to be that smart it can, of course, be reassuring. But on another more important level, it's always disappointing."*

But it's different enough

It's sufficiently different that you should not underestimate it. As many leaders who have got the top job, having worked up through the organization, say: *"It does look very different from different angles."* Janet

Gaymer is Commissioner for Public Appointments, having been Senior Partner at City of London law firm Simmons & Simmons. She says of her promotion to Senior Partner: *"I completely underestimated how different it would look from the top. I thought I knew it so well having worked in the firm for many years. But it does look different – and the relationships are different too."* When you move out of your core and start to operate across an organization, the same thing happens – and you need to change the way you lead accordingly. The same applies if you move out of your organization and into the "society" circle.

Richard Bowker is Group Chief Executive of National Express Ltd. Prior to this, he was Chief Executive of Partnerships for Schools and, before that, Chief Executive of the Strategic Rail Authority (SRA). So he has moved in and out of the private and public sectors. As he says of his move from the private sector to the SRA: *"It took a while to understand what a different world I was in. In business, the default currency is money. It may be the individual's or the shareholders' money, but it's basically money. In politics, it is power. You discover what the default currency is by watching what people do when it is under threat. In business, there is commitment to corporate social responsibility, values, and people development, but the whole lot will be dropped if the share value comes under threat. In politics, it's different. I have no doubt that every politician wakes up in the morning with a high degree of integrity and passion to produce change. But their default comes when their power is threatened. What's the point in having policies if you have no power? Do you know any politicians who would happily be in opposition?"*

Douglas Miller is Chair of the European Venture Philanthropy Association, after many years as a very successful venture capitalist in both the USA and the UK. He says it is absolutely crucial: *"not to give leaders credibility outside their proven sphere of competence. Once they go beyond it, they need to prove themselves again. Only the most arrogant individual uses the credibility and even mystique of their success in one world to claim credibility in a new one. Leaderships skills are transferable to new areas to some extent. But first, you need to assess the landscape, understand the issues, become familiar with the power sources, and most importantly, understand the culture. This takes considerable time and commitment."* You can hear the military man coming through this. Doug learnt a lot about leadership (as he says, *"hundreds of years ago"*) when he was in the Special Forces in Vietnam.

He has more good advice about assessing risks when you get to the outer circles: *"Don't always go for what other people say are the risks to watch out for: always assess them yourself. In Vietnam, I learnt pretty fast that the greatest risk was being around incompetent troops and commanders. So I reckoned that I should keep out of the general army, where the less competent and less trained guys were, and go into Special Forces where, though it might appear to be higher risk due to the types of missions involved, you were with the most competent guys, so the risks were greatly reduced."*

Appreciate the differences

As we have seen the partnerships multiply in the UK over the last ten years or so, we have also seen a great period of bringing in private sector leaders. Almost every civic agenda has produced a partnership or task force with a heavy private sector input. Sadly, in many cases, they have come in weighed down by the burden of great expectations – and then been aggrandized by the pedestal they have been put on. It is hard to move across circles at the best of times; but it is even harder when the expectations are so high. Too often, these leaders have not understood the world they were moving into and tried to introduce an order that is familiar to them. Or they have taken too long to understand the world they have walked into – and missed the boat as a result. They were simply not allowed the time to acclimatize. Some, however, have fallen for the flattery and seen no need to adapt. They are simply blind to both the differences and the merits of the new world. They sometimes even sneer at whatever they are not familiar with.

Here's a small but perhaps telling example. It's very hard to get senior leaders, private sector or not, to fill in an application form when they are applying for a public appointment. It's even harder when it's an equal opportunities form. They say: *"It's ridiculous. Look at what I have achieved over the years. This form is political correctness gone mad."* They don't take the time to ask why the form is there and what it is for. They don't consider that, in a democracy, maybe it is quite important to allow everyone to apply for appointments. So they simply will not fill in the form. Until recently, I was an Independent Assessor of Public Appointments, there to ensure fair play. More than once, I looked at application forms that were full of empty pages, bar the final signature. They didn't even bother to print their names underneath.

Sue Stapely is a solicitor and reputation management consultant at

Quiller Consultants, where she does much pro bono work for people who get into serious trouble. Her advice to me was: *"Don't look at applicants who refuse to fill in forms. They won't acclimatize."* She is also on the board of the Royal Court Theatre in London and draws a nice parallel: *"Think about the great actors. Don't trust the ones who won't audition. The greats always will – and they will play small parts in great plays too."*

Legitimacy

The legitimacy issue is one that might make the outer circles feel very, very different too. Within the organization, people are likely to howl: *"By what right does he or she stomp around and butt into everyone else's business and get in the way and question what we do?"* This happens whether the chief executive is passionate about encouraging people to lead beyond authority or not. Out in the society circle, you will get the same response from the experts and professionals. You will also get a variation from those who think democracy is only about elections – about going to the ballot box and voting and then leaving it all to politicians: *"By what right do you interfere here? Who elected him? What democratic legitimacy does she have? How dare they ask questions?"* On the whole, we have persuaded ourselves that the only form of legitimacy in an organization is by appointment, and, in a democracy, by election.

A couple of years ago, I was at a meeting in Belfast, looking at homelessness in the province. There was a man in the corner who kept on muttering: *"What is our legitimacy?"* We ignored him for a while, but eventually it got us down and I turned to him and said: *"In this room are the ten people who have done the most for homeless people in Northern Ireland over the last ten years. They did not sit at home watching the news and muttering. Nor did they demand that their politicians sort it out. Here and now, they are not discussing public policy, nor are they allocating public funds. They are simply thinking what they can do next – themselves. That is their legitimacy. It's a highly democratic legitimacy and it's a glorious one."*

Maybe we do too much equating of citizenship with rights and not enough with standing up. It can be hard to stand up. Last winter, I watched one of my children in our street. Someone walked along and dropped some rubbish on the pavement. Rachel ran after him to give it back and he turned on her and bellowed (as only adults who consider children irrelevant can) that she was undermining his democratic right to litter. Simon Fanshawe is an author and broad-caster – and a very active citizen in Brighton. His advice is: *"Get used to it. People will constantly question your legitimacy. The answer is, I'm someone whose bottom is no longer on the seat."*

Nelson Mandela is said to have pinned this powerfully: *"Our deepest fear is not that we are inadequate. Our deepest fear is that we are powerful beyond measure. It is our light, not our darkness, that most frightens us. We ask ourselves: who am I to be brilliant, gorgeous, talented, fabulous? Actually, who are you not to be? You are a child of God. Your playing small does not serve the world. There is nothing enlightened about shrinking so that other people won't feel insecure around you. We are all meant to shine, as children do. We were born to make manifest the glory of God that is within us. It is not just in some of us; it is in everyone. And, as we let our own light shine, we unconsciously give other people permission to do the same. As we are liberated from our own fear, our presence automatically liberates others."*

When you do stand up, just be prepared for what Diana Parker calls *"the brutality of questioning when you move out of your core circle."* Be prepared too for criticism (and worse) from "experts" when, as an outsider, you tread on their turf. This was a revelation for me when I started working, with others, on issues to do with the media a couple of years ago. The project came about because a number of us felt that there was something seriously wrong in the relationship between the media and the citizen. It was a problem that very few people asked questions about because it was dangerous territory.

The history of this issue is littered with people who have argued for the media to get its house in order, only for their careers to falter as a result. If anything, we were motivated by the opposite approach: that, if things don't change soon, we will eventually end up with some form of externally imposed control of the media – maybe even legislation – which would be very unlikely to work. But, more importantly, it would curb an incredibly important piece of our democracy.

What this work has shown me is that it is very much easier to lead beyond authority when you do it as I always had previously. Until we began working with the media, I had always created something in an area of the outer circle where nothing else existed. Common Purpose, for example, was a new idea. I was not stepping on anyone's toes or incurring their wrath; I was building something out of nothing. It is very much harder to lead beyond your authority when you are moving outside your own core circle – but into someone else's.

One leader's outer circle is another leader's core

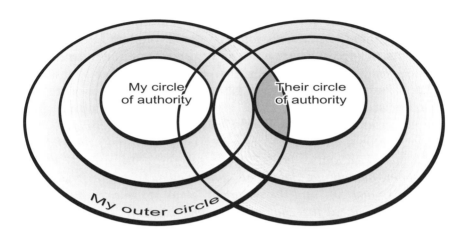

Until then, my legitimacy had occasionally been questioned by some old-style politicians with strange ideas that democracy was about politicians alone, and by some people who had laughed at my ideas in the early days. Now my legitimacy was being questioned in a big way – by some pretty powerful people who did not like outsiders asking questions. Over the last year, our questions have consistently been met, either indirectly or overtly, with another one: *"What do you know about the media – and by what right are you asking these questions anyway?"* The answer – that I am a citizen standing up – has not really passed muster. One key player simply told me I was a member of the chattering classes (I still don't quite understand what's wrong with chattering, by the way – it's better than silence). A clever man in television news helped enormously at one stage by explaining: *"You need to understand that most journalists don't think there is a problem. And the few that do, don't think there's a solution."* So we set up the Media Standards Trust, a group comprising both citizens and leaders from the media, to try and come up with some answers.

But it is interesting how hard it is to keep going when your legitimacy is constantly in question (and your motives are suspected) because this is not your area of expertise. You begin to lose sight of the objective and the rationale yourself. I don't cower easily – but I did recently. I met one of the biggest figures in regional newspapers at a party. He took me to pieces, I stuttered pathetically, then retired, full of rage. Luckily, across the room, was one of the big media supporters of the Trust. It was only after several minutes of him putting me back together that I felt able to face my attacker again. As he saw me coming, he gathered ready for another onslaught: *"Tell me the name of one editor of a major newspaper who would agree with you,"* he said. I told him I would email him a link to a recent article written by the editor of *The Independent.* The following morning, I did just that. But there was no response.

Lord Puttnam, President of UNICEF (UK) and advisor to the Department of Education, and a former filmmaker, would never let himself get into such a silly fight. He says: *"You cope with the legitimacy issue by doing your homework. As an advisor to the Department of Education, I visited more schools than anyone else. I remember hearing an interview with Paula Radcliffe, the long-distance runner. She said there were all kinds of clever training techniques but that, in the end, the fundamental issue was how many miles a week you do."*

It doesn't matter how long you've been out there, or how confident you are, you will meet hostility when you encroach on other people's ground. You've just got to be prepared for it.

Both leading beyond your authority and foreign travel can be very tough. Especially in hostile territory. Even when your passport is entirely in order, you're holding the right visa, and you have every right to be there.

ANALYSIS: THE SOURCES OF POWER

As you lead beyond authority, you are using many familiar approaches and skills – they are not new. John Rose summarized for me what he thought a good leader had, whether inside or beyond authority:

"Leadership – in and out of authority – takes courage; a broad view; common sense; a small ego; the ability to focus and concentrate effort; a preparedness to change your mind publicly for the right reasons; and an ability to engage and influence people."

This feels like a pretty good list, and John is right – it fits both situations (though maybe the last of his requirements is even more important in the outer circles). Most of the difference is of emphasis and degree – but these differences can be enormous.

Let us say that, as a leader, you can call on a variety of powers in any situation. Let's look at eight of them and see how you can apply them differently, and to different degrees, whether you are leading in or beyond authority.

- ❑ *The power of position.* This comes with the position you hold, that you were appointed or elected to, or that you have created for yourself.
- ❑ *The power of personality.* This comes from your strength of character, your "pizzazz," the energy you generate around you because of who you are as a person.
- ❑ *The power of ideas.* This is acquired through the quality of your ideas, your creativity.
- ❑ *The power of intellect.* This is your brainpower, analytical ability, capacity to grasp facts and put them into order.
- ❑ *The power to communicate.* This is your ability to get across an idea or message in a way which resonates for people, both individually and in groups.
- ❑ *The power to connect.* This is the power you gain if you are able to see connections and overlaps and use your networks to bring all the pieces together.
- ❑ *The power to invest.* Money talks. This power comes if you can invest resources or cash.
- ❑ *The power to reward.* This comes from your ability to reward people financially or through recognition. Part of this power is also the freedom to remove people from situations where they are not succeeding.

So you have these powers. But their effectiveness (and, frankly, usefulness) in influencing and inspiring those you seek to lead changes quite dramatically depending on which circle you are operating in:

	In authority (core circle)	Beyond authority (outer circles)
Power of position	85 percent	10 percent

In the core circle, this power is high because you have been given authority. It comes with budgets and resources, and you are directly accountable for their best use. It is not 100 percent, because there will always be limiting factors (some internal, some external). In the outer circles, even if you have been appointed to a role (leading a partnership for example, or becoming a non-executive director), it will be a position which comes with limited authority. You probably only really have the ultimate "power of position": being able to resign.

Power of personality	60 percent	90 percent

In the core circle, this power can be high but it does not have to be. Because you can make up for lack of "personality power" with others – especially the "power of position." In the outer circles, given that people are not obliged to follow you in the same way, you will need a great deal of "personality power."

Power of ideas	80 percent	90 percent

In the core circle, this is slightly higher than "personality power" because you won't be able to stay in most positions without ideas. But again, it does not have to be high, because you have other powers to compensate (particularly "position"). In the outer circles however, the ideas have to be good for people to believe in them and follow you. Though personality can cover for lack of "ideas power" for a while, it won't be enough if the ideas are not also there.

Power of intellect	90 percent	60 percent

In the core circle, which is a more structured environment, this is very important. In the less structured outer circles, it is still important – but less so. However, you will need intellect to cope with the complex equations you will encounter in the outer circles.

Power of communication   60 percent   100 percent
In the core circle, as with "personality power" and "ideas power," you won't be able stay in most positions without the ability to communicate. But again, the other powers can compensate if this is not your strength. Here, it is also much easier to delegate the communication to experts. In the outer circle, communication is vital. Just as intellectual rigor is less important in the outer circle, the importance of "communication power" soars.

Power to connect   40 percent   100 percent
In the core circle, the ability to connect is not as important – unless your organization is determined to break the silo culture. In the outer circles, your ability to use networks and make connections is critical.

Power to invest   80 percent   80 percent
In all the circles, money gives you power. But it is often just the power to gain compliance, rather than to get the most from people.

Power to reward   90 percent   10 percent
In the core circle, you are usually paid. This is one of the strongest reasons why people stick within their core circle. You also don't have to suffer fools gladly – because you can move them (out, or sideways). In the outer circles, some roles might be paid or recognized in a bonus, but not all of them. (Some people might argue that this figure should be a negative one for the outer circles, since the risks are often high and the rewards sometimes intangible.) Out here, you have to learn to work with people you don't rate, because they are not yours to "move."

A couple of years ago, I met a man who ran a hedge fund in the City of London, whom everyone was attempting to persuade to chair a very important development company in his home region. The first words he barked at me were: *"So what is the business case?"* I said: *"There isn't one."* He barked again: *"What will I get out of it?"* I responded: *"Nothing, maybe a big headache."* He paused and looked angry: *"So why should I do it?"* There was no other answer than *"Because you have to. Who else would do it better? It is incredibly important. What are they going to write on your gravestone?"*

There are rewards in the outer circles. But perhaps not ones we can always measure in percentages.

PART 4

So what should you leave behind?

For a moment, put yourself in the shoes of someone who is looking for a leader who can operate beyond his or her authority. You've identified a task but, as chief executive, you know it's not an issue you can resolve from the top, and you know it does not belong to a single division or function. You also know that it needs someone with energy and the ability to work right across the organization. You can back the right person and give encouragement, but you can't clear the way. You think that there is someone who would have the passion to take it on (it may even be the person who first brought the issue to your attention). But: does that person have the right frame of mind – and the right set of skills – to do it?

I think you only know if you have chosen well when he/she leaves the room after the briefing. The person you need to be worried about is the one who asks: "How much budget will I have? How many people will be working for me on this? What will my job title be?" And, finally: "How will my efforts be recognized?"

The people who get your heart running faster, who make you excited and longing to go out of the door with them, are the ones who just leave the room after saying "yes." And then, just as they go out, they pop their head back through the door and say: *"Oh, if I need people, or a title, or a budget, I'll come back to you."* It is not that they forgot to ask, or that they need some time to assess the task and calculate the necessary resources. It is because their first instinct is that they don't need the authority that all these things imply. And their second thought is that, even if they have all this, it might actually get in the way.

Ask any of the leaders who are great at working beyond their authority and they will tell you that, if you have a budget, everyone will be trying to get a piece of it. And, in any case, budgets often only come with agendas that have been set in advance.

Sometimes, it's better to travel light. So, before we look at what you need, let's look at what you need to leave behind.

Jettison 1: giving instructions

There are plenty of organizations where leaders, even within their authority, can't just tell people what to do. But, out here, you really can't do it. To anyone. At all. Ever.

Janet Gaymer's law firm, like almost all professional service firms, is a partnership. So she was running an organization where the leader has less authority than most. Which is probably why she has a clearer view than most of what it takes to lead beyond authority in the outer circles: *"With a partnership, you are always balancing consultation with direction. It's like keeping a plane in balance, with consultation and direction as the two wings. If you get the balance wrong, either way, it takes quite a long time to get back to where you were. And, of course, there is the real danger that you will drop out of the sky. The best indicator that you are out of kilter is when people start objecting to lots of things and eventually you get stuck. It's worth treating everything as a long march with a vote at the end. It is not a question of simply taking people with you, you have to actually obtain their active vote."*

(Janet tells me that Harvard Business School considers that one of the hardest jobs is to lead professional firms like hers, because the shareholders – who elsewhere are normally outside the organizational fence – are partners, and therefore involved in the day-to-day running of the firm. Coalition-building and negotiation are the order of the day. Which is why, in organizations like this, leading beyond authority skills are so important, even within authority.)

John Inge is Bishop of Huntingdon. He was on the very first Common Purpose program we ran, in Newcastle in 1989. He describes a conversation he once had with a senior Army officer who believed that leadership was all about moral courage. John disagreed: *"It seems to me that, crucial though this is, there also is the small matter of persuading others to do what you believe to be right. I now realize that this was an issue rather more for me, because I generally have to lead beyond authority – whereas he gave orders that had to be obeyed."*

Dame Anita Roddick, the founder of The Body Shop, was the first Chair of the Common Purpose trustees. She knew an enormous amount about leading without authority – you learn it the hard way when you run a franchise operation. You can't tell anyone much, so you learn good habits: *"The only way to control a franchise operation is to make the center so unbelievably good that no one would wish to do without it."* I have never forgotten this. As Common Purpose has grown, we have always put an inordinate amount of effort into the making the center strong – providing strong services (particularly information technology), and ensuring that the ideas are always one step ahead.

There will always be huge areas, big gaps (even in the most structured of environments), where you have no authority at all. *"The difference is that, in the outer circles, the gap is total,"* says Chris Mathias. Chris has spent most of his career successfully running businesses and financing new ventures, and is now a partner at CMG Partners and Arbor Ventures. But he also has experience as a "venture philanthropist" in the charitable sector. As he says: *"Even in the big organizations, with highly professional employees, it's like leading volunteers because you are not paying people enough to stay just for the money."*

As so many people out here will tell you, you can't instruct. But people do. Because it's so very hard not to. You slide back to the instincts that serve you well in the core, because it's irresistible. You want to get things done, and it's taking so long, and the coalitions are driving you mad, so you cry out "let's just tell them." But it never works. Stranger Two is the Chairman of an enormous company in the UK. As he says: *"You coach leaders to lead beyond authority – and you have to tempt them slowly. Sometimes they promise they will never stamp their authority again. They promise, a bit like alcoholics, that they won't. That, next time, when the going gets tough, they won't ride a coach and horses through things. But then they weaken – and they do it. If they are still within their authority, they get away with it. But there is always a lasting resentment. If they start handing out instructions beyond their authority, they have already lost."*

Some people simply can't get their heads around this idea at all. I think of two of my daughters speaking one evening. Rachel, aged 12, was trying to organize a fashion show, involving all her school year, to raise funds for a teenage AIDS project in London. Although most 12-year-old girls are interested in clothes and make up, the boring bits about actually making it happen weren't anything like as easy to get her classmates excited about. She sat, frustrated, and her older sister Kate (whose experience of leadership is entirely based on captaining almost every sports team she has ever been part of) advised her: *"Just tell them to do it."* Rachel, with no authority, knows full well that she can't tell anyone what to do, but she just cannot get Kate to understand this.

There will always be leaders who can't get their heads around the lack of authority in the outer circles. They are better staying in their core circle. Otherwise, they tend to create structures and unreal microcosms of power in the outer circles – and everyone around them simply keeps out of their way. Zenna Atkins, long experienced in leading beyond her authority, pins it well: *"This is why many leaders who, in their own space, are seen as driven, empowering, and motivating become bullying, domineering, and aggressive out of it. Yet they may well be using the same skills."*

In a nutshell, as Ned Sullivan says: *"If you can't listen with empathy and see things from others' positions, if you make quick decisions and behave as you do in the inner circle, giving instructions, nothing will happen."*

Jettison 2: intellectual rigor

You also have to accept that intellectual rigor is not as important in an unstructured environment. It is still important and must not be left behind entirely. But, if you lead predominantly from the head – and if you aim to win every fight from the head – you will realize quite rapidly that you become irrelevant. I have sat with many highly intelligent leaders and looked back on what happened when they first moved beyond their authority (for some, both their first and last taste of such activity). Some write the experience off entirely, muttering *"they are all irrational and amateur and impossible, so what could I do?"* as they scramble back into their core circle. Others talk about discovering – too late – that they were playing chess when, all around them, others were playing backgammon (sometimes not even backgammon, but pretty dirty pool). And, because it was all so unfamiliar, they fell back on their core instincts: they set about producing a rational, intelligent piece of work – which had no impact at all.

Lord Simon used to be Chair and Chief Executive of BP. He has a good theory of why this happens: *"Many leaders in the UK and France studied Classics. This teaches you that it's all about analysis and rationality. You make a rational case, you lay it out, and that's it. In the old days, that's what I did; the case was accepted because it was rational. If you are in an organization that sets out to achieve simple tasks, it works well. You assimilate a strategy, communicate, and deliver it. There are many people who stick to this and produce huge success in their core area."*

Chris Mathias has a different model for what works: *"In the past,*

I always did the analytical thing, and it's not that this is not the right response – often it is what's called for – but it is only part of the picture. I used to think that the main challenge was to produce a cogent, defensible case, based on facts and good data. Now I turn things around, and discuss them and look at them from all the angles in the belief that, by playing with the issue, the answer will come. And that, [if people find] it together, it will be far more powerful."

Philip Kolvin is a barrister, based at the Inns of Court in London. In1998, he took on the role of Chair of the Crystal Palace Campaign to save the historic site of the 1851 Great Exhibition from destruction and conversion into a multiplex cinema:

"The biggest revelation for me was that, as a barrister, I thought in straight lines – but this just did not work in an unstructured environment. I had been taught to identify the target and then simply get there. I had never thought about the soft stuff. People come to my chambers to see me and ask for my advice, and I tell them: 'You do this, and this and this and then you get here,' and they say, 'Thank you, Mr. Kolvin.' At work, this is what people are used to, and this is what their bosses are used to. But, with volunteers over whom you have no authority and with whom you have no relationship, it's different. Why hadn't I seen this before? Because that's what I learned at school. Education reduces things to a logical order: water falls, poems rhyme, dramas have resolution. Yet the world isn't like this. It's confused and messy and edgy. Command and control doesn't work. But the soft skills for me simply didn't translate, and I had no idea how to operate in an unstructured environment, never mind lead in it.

I came to the campaign too late, so it had all gone too far already. Planning permission had already been granted. My first instinct was to mount a legal challenge. I raised loads of money for it, appointed poor barristers, and the legal action went all wrong. The result was that I had wasted loads of people's money, I had lost the campaign, my reputation as a barrister was shot, as was my reputation in the community, and worst of all, I had no idea what to do next. I went for a run and then threw myself on my bed, utterly miserable. Then I sat bolt upright: what we had to do was lawful direct action, a boycott. I realized that the legal, rational argument was not the only piece of the puzzle (although, in passing, it did buy us nine months to build up our resources). What we needed was a cascade of methods, not just the rational case. Looking back, two-thirds of what we came up with worked. Some were brilliant, some OK, some were rubbish, but they did engage the community. Prior to that, all [local people] had done was pay for the legal challenge.

It became about people: about their frustrations, their anger. You had to assemble them all. You needed it to rain with ideas and projects, but then, when the rain hits the ground, you can't lose it. You have to catch it and channel it. That's what we did, and we won."

Dr Musharraf Hussain is Director General of Bobbersmill Community Centre in Nottingham, and an Imam. He is well versed in leading beyond authority because, as he says, Imams have no authority outside their own community: *"We made a bid for our school to be supported by the Local Education Authority in Nottingham – and we failed. It is interesting, looking back, as I think I became blinded by the strength of the arguments we were making in our bid. There was such an overwhelming and strong case and the need was clear. Maybe I relied too much on the intellectual argument. In fact, I was dazzled by it. With hindsight, I realize that the case was only part of the picture. The piece we did not put enough effort into was the building of the relationships."*

The same message comes from Richard Bowker: *"The outer circle is a world of utter ambiguity. For businessmen to be successful in it, they almost have to take a sort of drug. They will see obvious and perfectly rational and logical solutions to problems. But others will see equally obvious and rational alternative solutions that are very different. They are not of lesser logic but it's a different logic and coming from a different starting point. Business people find it difficult to see these competing logics. And they fail when they are blind about the fact that they are blind to them. Take an example: The West Coast Mainline project was running massively over budget; it had become a £13 billion project that was out of control. I did a rational assessment of the task. It appeared self-evident that you had to put most of the money into the bottom third of the customer base. Here you would use capital to greatest effect and you would satisfy the most number of customers. But the Scots would not back this, however logical. They needed to see money spent in Scotland: on Scottish turf with Scottish staff. It was not that they could not see the rational argument I was making, but it was unsellable for them. So you had to sub-optimize the plan, just a bit, to gain their support."*

So intellectual rigor is part of the picture – but nothing like as big a part as it is inside authority.

Jettison 3: strict hierarchies

You need to leave behind the temptation to see power in structures and hierarchies. And you need to get used to looking for power in less obvious places.

As Tom Frawley says: *"Don't always look for the power at the top – maybe there is a guy in the middle. He will be interested in everything, will always know the right places to be: in the middle of things. He is likely to be quite invisible, hugely well networked, but very few people will recognize his power. He is there at every debate, he is a great listener and probably wonderful company, and he knows the system back to front. He is the guy you are after."*

As I observe leaders beyond their authority, they often miss out on where the power really is. They are brought up to look for power at the top and need to discover the value of the margins. Some very sound advice was given to me by a former Chef de Cabinet at the European Commission. He observed that it took leaders too long to discover where it was all really happening. And by the time they did, it was usually time for them to leave Brussels anyway.

Most leaders also underestimate the power that can lurk in unfamiliar places. The further out of the circles you go, the less obvious the sources of power will be. Vast budgets can be under the control of what appear to be very junior people. And, in some cases, not just junior people, but people with no job title at all. Susan Liautaud is, among other things, an Associate Dean at Stanford Law School in the USA. But the title does not say much and, outside of Stanford, she seldom uses it. She regrets that so few people recognize that: *"Not all leaders have job titles."* Because do not be misled: in some ways, Susan is one of the most powerful leaders beyond authority I know. Her influence comes from her ability, her networks across the USA, UK, and France, and from the wide radar screen she scans because of the many worlds she moves between. If you have a chance to share ideas with her and get her on your side, you'd be foolish not to take it. Even at the expense of people with job titles to die for.

Immense influence can be wielded by "ideas people" or good communicators. Great ideas can come from cultures that wouldn't even be heard within many organizations. It gets even more difficult when you have to answer to an authority that is unfamiliar to you. As David Varney says: *"When you meet authority that is strong but unfamiliar, your first response is almost that of a teenager: 'you have power over me, which I resent.' And you decide that the best way to deal with it is to demean it."*

I met a Common Purpose graduate who explained the principle of "power in strange places" after he had come back from his summer holiday. He said that, on the flight back, he had had a "Common Purpose moment." The flight attendant came up and asked him if his son would like to go up and see the cockpit. He said yes please – and could he come too? It was a night flight, so they went from the well-lit cabin into the darkened cockpit, where the Captain and co-pilot were sitting, entirely in control. The air was different – it smelt of stale coffee. He found himself in someone else's territory, and it felt deeply unfamiliar and uncomfortable. He began to ask about the buttons and the lights on the instrument panel. The pilot explained that many of them were fitted for an old model of the plane and didn't actually work. In fact, some buttons were actually lights. If you didn't know, you could sit there pressing buttons – and nothing would ever happen. Some buttons were wired together behind the panel so, if you hit one, another light started flashing at you, from the other side. The temptation to get back into the light and the clean air, the familiar territory, was compelling. It was the sense of being irrelevant, of not having a clue, that terrified him. It reminded him of times during the program when the temptation to quit and run was huge. Of how, over the months, he had learned to keep going and keep learning. But that it took a long time to assess which buttons to hit, and which to ignore. It took time, also, to learn that it was important to look for the right ones, not just the biggest, or the closest to the center – or the ones that shone the brightest.

Within authority, the structures tend to be clearer and there is some indication that, the further up people go, the more power they have. So you instinctively aim to influence the top and not look at the margins. I can think of many hugely frustrated leaders, way beyond their authority, hitting away at a button and getting utterly furious that nothing happened. They just did not realize that it wasn't wired up, or it was for an old model, or it didn't keep the plane in the air but just switched on the light in the lavatories.

So forget strict hierarchies. And maybe even actual job titles. Zenna Atkins says she is always fascinated to observe the leaders who struggle to cope at OpenGround gatherings (which are run by Common Purpose). These are day-long meetings of about 100 people, all leaders of civil society who are increasingly addressing issues that are not local, but national. We hold the sessions every year, to help build and connect civil society across the UK. At this level, so few of the participants seem to know each other. In fact, they seem to form opinions about each other from what they read in the newspapers. When they get together, they gather round big national issues of the day which they feel need addressing. Zenna says the participants who can't figure out how to use the opportunity are those who *crave clear outcomes* and, most importantly, find it very uncomfortable "*not having their job titles on their name badges."* Because their job title automatically indicates their authority to anyone close enough to see it. And they can't assess anyone else without this important piece of information. Tom Frawley talks about every sector having its own "virility test." Apparently, if you run a psychiatric ward, you tell other people how many beds you have or, if you are a radiologist, how many CAT scanners you control. Like the name-tag, it's shorthand for your level of authority, your sense of your own importance.

Bill Knight was Janet Gaymer's predecessor as Senior Partner at Simmons & Simmons. He is now Chair of the Financial Reporting Review Panel. He has been fascinated by the experience of retirement: *"You go into shock and discover how little you have learnt. When people ask you what you do, you tell them what you used to be. It takes months to adjust – just like a bereavement."* If you go beyond your authority, maybe you just have to do the grieving earlier.

Some are luckier; they have not had to grieve for lost structure or authority, because they never had it in the first place. As John Rose says: *"I was lucky that I came in late to Rolls-Royce, not in the normal graduate entry, at a time when that was unusual. So, in the early years, I never did a job that already existed. I wasn't conscious of the hierarchy. The only way I could achieve anything was through influence. I was lucky that I didn't know what could not be done. I learnt that it was not just about having the right idea: you had to influence and persuade and you needed others to be on board if you wanted to achieve anything, and I had to trust people. As a result, I became more collegial. In a complex business, you need to have a coalition of support and skills."*

Yearning to have no structure can be as debilitating as grieving for one you have lost. Indeed, leaders who don't want any structure at all in the outer circles may find that they get what they wish for. As Roisín McDonough (who has long experience of the peace movement in Northern Ireland) warns: *"We got caught up in the tyranny of structurelessness. We rejected hierarchy, we ridiculed traditional forms of power. We built networks: allegedly egalitarian ones, spontaneous groupings. You got a new kind of tyranny. While pretending to equality and that all decisions could be reversed, we ended up with the dominance of the loudest voice."*

Jettison 4: the instinct to tidy

Resist the temptation to tidy things up, to make things simple. Because they aren't. Too many leaders equate complexity with untidiness – and believe that tidying will create simplicity. They cope with being in the cockpit, in strange territory, by making themselves busy and tidying up, and getting the captain to make it simple. Well, especially in the outer circles, it isn't.

I think of my mother when she visits us some days. Her house is beautiful and very tidy. Ours is not. It is also noisy and seems unfriendly sometimes, because everyone is rushing around with some plan, or task, or bath to turn off. She often starts to tidy up, because she cares and wants to help: cleaning windows, or hoovering, or ironing. At one level, of course, it is lovely. At another, you want to say, "*It is a mess – but sit down and listen to the chaos and you will feel more part of it and maybe see that, somewhere, there is even some sense in it.*" But the temptation to tidy is strong.

In the core circle, tasks tend to be simpler, more "tidyable." Let's face it, organizations (and, even more, divisions within organizations) are designed to deliver pretty simple and focused tasks. The challenges of the core circle are often relatively simple equations. To survive in the outer circles, you have to recognize – and even enjoy – complex multiple equations. Yet leaders too often decide that the lack of tidiness happens because, in the outer circles, people enjoy making it all more complex and are incapable of seeing things simply.

Lord (Adair) Turner is a director of Standard Chartered and Chair of the Pensions Commission. For him, the ultimate leader beyond authority is a Chief Constable: "*The very thought of being a Chief Constable is daunting. Balancing the competing views and agendas on your board, dealing with a media that is often out to get you, balancing long and short-term targets, dealing with the many, many stakeholders whose interests are so often conflicting. I don't know that I could do it.*"

If the targets are simpler in the core circle, so is the process of achieving them. Mostly, it's about assimilating, communicating, and delivering. In the private sector, it is even clearer – largely because the need for partnership with other organizations whose success is key to your own is significantly less. Lord (Paddy) Ashdown, former leader of the Liberal Democrat party and now in the House of Lords, puts it succinctly: "*Why are so many able and charismatic politicians blinded by successful businessmen? Because politicians long for the simplest of measurements. They long for a clear scorecard and, of course, it's much easier to measure the success of a businessman. Politicians crave simplicity and want to believe that things can be made simple. Also, especially as they get older, they get impatient; they can't bear going slowly. It's a natural human instinct to want to go faster.*"

Adair Turner agrees: *"I think many business leaders, while being great leaders in the business space, don't share that love of the specific complexities and difficulties of the political process. If they do get involved in public policy deliberations, they find the inherently political nature of the process frustrating, rather than intriguing. If I have been successful in at least some of my public policy roles, it may be because a bit of me is actually a politician at heart, rather than because I have brought business perspectives to bear on policy problems."*

Geoff Mulgan is Director of the Young Foundation and, prior to that, was Head of Policy at No. 10 Downing Street. He says: *"So many leaders arrived to tell us how simple it all really was. If I had a pound for every time I heard 'if you can't say it in one sentence, then it's not worth saying.' They seemed to think in PowerPoint presentations."* But simply tidying doesn't work beyond authority. Somehow, as with my mother, you have to take leaders aside and persuade them not to link complexity with messiness, and to resist the urge to tidy. Otherwise, they will miss the important points and end up tinkering with the wrong issues.

Jettison: but don't throw away

So these four instincts need to be jettisoned. It's not easy. It's also not as if you won't go back to them as you move between roles, and in and out of the circles. As Diana Parker says: *"You can't abandon the core. You have to be able to go in and out; you need to be known for your capacity to do both. You need to emanate outwards, while not abandoning the center."* Dame Deirdre Hutton is Chair of the Food Standards Agency. She agrees: *"Be very clear that you have to unlearn the leading inside authority approach. But you are only putting it aside, you are sure to need to pick it up again."*

And it has to be done with huge bravery. As Stranger Two says: *"Leaders do adapt to new situations, but it is with great difficulty that they abandon the characteristics and behaviors that have caused them to prosper to date. Successful people have a model of what works and what doesn't, and in what situations. They have done it before, and it has succeeded. It takes time to realize that it doesn't work in a new environment."*

If you don't jettison these instincts, you may not make the transition. You may well fail and, like so many other people who have tried and failed, retreat to the core circle and end up rubbishing the outer ones and claiming it was all a waste of time. But you may be wrong. In fact, there's every chance that, if you go out there with the wrong approach, you will be part of the problem.

SCENARIO: WHO SHOULD YOU BACK BEYOND AUTHORITY?

You run an organization. You have a "leading beyond authority" task that needs to be done. You have identified someone to take it on and briefed them carefully. You know you have chosen the wrong person if they say …

Tarek Ben Halim is Founder and Trustee of the Arab Learning Initiative and a former investment banker at Goldman Sachs.

> *"What exactly did you say?"*

I asked Manal to set up Arab Learning Initiative in Morocco. She had worked with ALI for three months in Egypt to see and learn how we do things. I carefully explained what she needed to do and the standards she had to aim for.

I realized that I had made a big mistake when I noticed her furiously scribbling down notes of what I was saying. I asked her what she was doing and she said she did not want to forget what I had said. It occurred to me that she was doing what she had been taught in her Egyptian school: how to memorize, not how to think.

Richard Bowker is Group Chief Executive of National Express Ltd, former Chief Executive of Partnerships for Schools and, prior to that, the Strategic Rail Authority.

> *"We must keep the board/politicians away from this."*

Anyone who said this would be too naïve for the task. You can't exclude the ultimate leaders of an organization (or country) because you have decided that they will "play politics." Leaders who try to do the task this way will just end up in a game of subterfuge. It won't work and they will get found out.

> *"We just need to get our heads down, make some decisions, kick some things into touch, and get on with it."*

These people would be too impatient. Because things don't work like this in the outer circle, where there is no authority and there are many players. You have to learn to finesse.

David Hill is Chief Executive of Ashford Borough Council, and former Secretary to the Royal Commission on the Reform of the House of Lords.

"I am sure I can push this one through."

They simply can't. They do not have the authority to do so and, if they assume that they have, they will fail.

"Give me a week to come up with a plan."

It's not a plan we need (and certainly not in a week). It's a process that will produce the result.

"How many staff will I have?"

If you want an army of staff in the outer circles, then all the other players will switch off and leave it to you. Then you will get stuck with the problem which has now become all yours.

"I know the solution!"

If you do, then keep it quiet. It is neither here nor there that you do. What you have to do is to get others to work it out for themselves so that they have ownership of the outcome. Of course it helps if you have an idea, because then you will make better judgments on the process, timing, and ideas. But, if you know the solution, keep it to yourself."

Oliver Nyumbu is Chief Executive of Caret Ltd.

I would worry most if they asked nothing.

To lead beyond authority, they will have to know how to ask questions. I have watched two managers in the same organization over the last six months. The first, with more zeal than wisdom, has consistently made bad use of questions and statements. He is seen as having taken on colleagues. During meetings, he has gone from raising concerns to rather unsubtle and unveiled personal attacks. Needless to say, he has not received thank-you cards for this behavior and remains frustrated that his suggestions are not taken up. Indeed, colleagues have begun to distance themselves, so they are not tarnished by his increasingly poisoned attitude. Moreover, when using questions, he rarely inquires to learn, but mainly seeks to prove himself right. Increasingly, this otherwise technically brilliant director is working well below his designated authority and potential influence.

The second has a rather different approach. He is well practiced in the art of kicking the ball, not the player. He is good at raising concerns and attacking issues without becoming unduly threatening. So what does he do well? He seems very aware of the fact that "in most conflicts, there is no shortage of words." As a consequence, he is good at suppressing his urge to confront and teach, preferring to use questions really well. The result? He has increasing influence on matters outside of his immediate responsibilities. Indeed, he has the CEO's ear on crucial issues of strategy. He leads beyond his authority.

PART 5

What position are you going to play in?

So, you're packed (and unpacked) and ready to go out to the outer circles. But first, you have to decide what role you're going to play. Or, if you're going to be yourself (never entirely a bad move out here), what position you're going to play in.

But, before that, you need to know who you're likely to meet. Because there will be some familiar faces – even in the most unfamiliar territory.

The usual suspects

You'll meet everyone you would expect to meet – because they cross all the circles and inhabit all the worlds. The "cynic," who gave up long ago, but hasn't stopped talking. The "grown-up," who sits on the sidelines and tells the rest of us to stop behaving like children. The "enthusiast," who is so excited to be in this new space and says "Won't it be great now that we are all together?" The "earnest," who thinks it's all so different, who will respect everything and everyone, especially the last person he spoke to, having left his judgment back in the core circle. The "you're so lucky to have me," who knows just how swanky she is so, of course, we will all follow her without her having to make any effort. The "Mr Chairman," who needs authority, so he brought some of it with him, creating a microcosm of his authority in the new world. The "busy," for whom all is meetings, process, and paper, with outcomes nowhere on the list. The "worried," who is terrified of stepping on anyone else's toes. The "complicator," who makes it an ever more difficult game. The "simplifier," who thinks it's just about tidying everything up. The "lost," who finds it hard to make anything happen. The "scripted," who is terrified by this new world – and paranoid about diverting from the script. The "ambitious," who knows what she wants out of this and intends to get it – for herself.

There are many more. None of which you want to become. They are all here and in many different combinations. Some succeed, others fail. At different times, different people in different configurations are useful, so some will have their moments. In the outer circles, many will simply have to be suffered or worked around because you don't have the authority to move them.

Picking positions

In the outer circles, there are four principal positions in which you can choose to play. And, before you go out there, you need to decide which to choose – and which to avoid – in which situations.

I call them "rebel," "transformer," and (borrowing a great East German phrase) "useful idiot" and "expert idiot." Rebels stand outside and demand change. Transformers produce change from the inside. Useful idiots, despite what may well be the best of intentions, allow themselves to be used by others. And expert idiots lack the general knowledge to be truly effective beyond their specialism.

Rebel

Tom Cummings is the Founding Partner of Executive Learning Partnership. Previously, he was Head of Leadership at Unilever. He now works with leaders across many of the biggest and most difficult (often because they are the biggest) organizations in the world. He says of rebels: "*We need rebels in organizations. They have passion – and they don't give up. They resonate, connect people, bug you. And they channel the energy in the organization to create change.*" Tom calls them "activists," but there are many expressions for them. Deirdre Hutton calls a specific kind of rebel "the remarkable person." She explains: "*I was very taken with this expression, which I came across at Shell. Of course, in a team you need everyone to be going in the same direction and all going down roughly the same tramlines. But you need someone looking the other way, who is not just a rebel but a remarkable person too, who asks 'Have you thought of ...?' I think that if you are any good as a leader, you will have performed the remarkable person role at some time, when you say 'I know I signed up to this idea, but I have a feeling I might have been wrong.' The trouble is that most people like a quiet life, so if there is a rationale for going with the herd, they will. To be a remarkable person, you need the courage to stand against the herd.*"

Shami Chakrabarti is Director of the civil rights organization Liberty. Many people think of her as a rebel because she is so frequently on television, making her case. Though passionate, it's always very well thought through and presented – that's why they remember her. She does not accept that she is a rebel. In fact, she is very tough on them: *"Rebels don't produce change, because they are fanning their own anger. They won't play the system, they are not self-deprecating enough, they don't seek to resonate, they find it hard to behave in a collegiate way, and they end up isolated too often. You have to learn to save your outrage and focus."* Simon Fanshawe, whose long list of leading beyond authority achievements includes being a founder of Stonewall, the gay rights organization in the UK, is tough too: *"Rebels are not prepared, in the end, to accept responsibility for a solution. They refuse to balance competing interests. Basically, they oppose rather than propose."*

But this may well be to underestimate the value of the rebel. Really effective rebels are perhaps much more clear-headed than is commonly thought. I spoke to human rights campaigner Peter Tatchell. He has led (and continues to lead) many campaigns, not just on behalf of the gay community, but against oppression wherever he sees it: *"I try to concentrate on issues others are not looking at. Amnesty International, for example, has focused attention on the abuses in Burma, but few human rights groups are doing anything about the slow genocide in West Papua."* Many journalists will tell you that Peter is more media-savvy than any politician they know. As he says: *"Before we had 24/7 media and the Internet, rebels relied on public meetings and leaflets. Now, I can send out an email simultaneously to 2,500 journalists across the world and have an instant impact. I have built up, over time, a reputation for doing campaigns in a way that is illuminating, interesting, and well thought through. I spend a lot of time researching and fact-checking. This makes for a more effective campaign. It also results in journalists coming to trust me as a source of credible, accurate, and reliable information."* Peter is absolutely clear that we need rebels: *"Rebels create the uproar and mayhem that helps break silences and invisibilities. They kick-start the process of reform. Their direct action protests are a catalyst for change."*

Peter is very methodical in his rebel role. To produce change he says: *"You need to:*

❑ *shame and embarrass the people who are in the way and/or who need to change*
❑ *present a moral and practical case for change that is well thought through*
❑ *build political alliances*
❑ *develop a network of sympathetic journalists*

- ❑ *produce clever, witty, informative, and entertaining campaigns*
- ❑ *harass and wear down the opponents of change, so that they decide that defending the status quo is not worth the hassle – that it's easier to go with you*
- ❑ *present credible alternative policies; you can't just be negative."*

An example was his campaign against Robert Mugabe, though it took a slightly unpredicted turn: *"Standard military theory says you never fight a battle you cannot win, but sometimes it can be worth sustaining a degree of defeat if, in the process, you mortally wound an opponent. The battle to bring President Mugabe to justice is a good example. We had tried to get him arrested for crimes against humanity through the usual legal means, but there is a diplomatic convention that gives 'sovereign immunity' to heads of state. This lets off the hook some of the world's worst human rights abusers. Since the courts were not going to act, I decided to get Mugabe by carrying out a citizen's arrest. The first time was in 1999 in London. Together with my OutRage! colleagues, I ambushed his motorcade and actually seized him. The second time was in 2001 in Brussels, in the lobby of the Hilton hotel. His bodyguards beat me unconscious. The headlines all over the world were about what Mugabe's henchmen had done to a peaceful protestor, in front of the media, in a European capital, in broad daylight. It prompted many people to conclude that Mugabe was probably doing even worse things back in Zimbabwe when the world wasn't watching. Being beaten up was not part of the plan, but it helped expose the brutality of the Mugabe regime. I still have some slight brain and eye damage. But we caused his reputation far greater damage."*

Transformer

Transformers are the people who see change through. David Simon remembers watching the great transformers as they emerged at BP, where he was Chairman and Chief Executive: *"They broke the boundaries because they were change makers. What was exciting was watching when their enthusiasm for the outer rim began to show through and it became clear that they cared about problems other than their own. The most successful ones were those who stayed at the table the longest and saw things through. They also figured out how to legitimize their ideas, policies, and ideologies."* Roisín McDonough says she loves the transformers: *"Most of us plod along, thinking we are doing OK. Then something happens or the underlying trends reveal an opportunity. The transformer recognizes the opportunity, has been building up the skills to do it for some time, and seizes it. It's lovely to watch."*

Janet Paraskeva has recently left the Law Society, where she was Chief Executive, to become the First Commissioner of the Civil Service Commission. Janet is a transformer. Some would describe her as a rebel (at least, a former rebel), but she would deny this emphatically: *"I have never been a rebel because I have always chosen to be in the system."* She rejects the idea that you have to make such a stark choice anyway. *"I believe in change from the inside, and I don't believe that, just because you get into the center of power, you inevitably become part of it. I don't think you should ever stay out of things on principle. Too many opportunities are missed as a result of this attitude. Don't join things if you feel deeply uncomfortable about them, or if you know you are going to be eaten up. But otherwise produce change from within."*

"Useful idiot"

Hans Reckers is a board member of Deutsche Bundesbank (and board member of Common Purpose in Germany). He introduced me to this East German expression. Useful idiots take the view that it is better to stay in post and try to affect what is going on around them from within, and they think they should continue to do so almost at all cost. They add credibility, legitimacy, authority. By effectively lending the dictator their personal "brand" – a brand they will have no doubt worked hard to build and protect – they collude with tyranny, albeit in a passive way (and often unwittingly). The brand is what the dictator is so hungry to acquire, in return for leaving the useful idiot in office.

In the 1930s, for example, Von Papen was Hitler's Vice Chancellor in the Weimar Republic. Apparently, even on his deathbed, he was convinced that he had been right to stay in post. He thought he could control Hitler and steer Germany through the chaos of the early 1930s. I suspect that history judges him differently. He survived the war and its aftermath, and lived until the 1960s (pretty much the most severe penalty he received was having his driving license confiscated). One thinks of Martin Luther King: *"We will have to repent in this generation not merely for the hateful words and actions of the bad people, but for the appalling silence of the good people."* Unfortunately, useful idiots do more than say nothing: their passivity gives the dictator tacit support which he or she is only too happy to use to advantage.

I don't think it is just dictators who need useful idiots (or find them useful). Almost all leaders will benefit from a useful idiot here and there. Someone to appear to be taking action – the noisier the better – whom the person in power knows full well will not see it through. Or who will get tied up in an issue or will simply not realize what the real game is. By appointing a useful idiot to deal with a difficult issue, the leader will appear to be acting on it, but will in fact prevent others from acting. The useful idiot creates the illusion of activity in an area that the leader might prefer to avoid (or keep on hold) at the moment. Lord (Chris) Patten is Chancellor of both Oxford University and Newcastle University. Among his many previous roles, he was Governor of Hong Kong. He is enlightening – and scathing – on the danger of useful idiots. As he says: "*The most dangerous useful idiots are the ones who have huge legitimacy (and therefore authority) but lack either wisdom or courage. They have convinced themselves that their role is never to 'make the conduct of the Queen's business more difficult.' Their ultimate loyalty is unswervingly to the smooth running of the State.*"

The thought of being a useful idiot is mortifying to everyone I've ever mentioned it to. To finally break out of your core circle, only to discover that you are being used as a pawn? Unthinkable. But it happens a lot. To a lot of leaders.

Expert idiot

Then there are expert idiots – another useful German expression (and a variant on useful idiot). These are leaders who know a huge amount about a small, sometimes tiny, core circle. Sometimes they are catapulted from the very inner circle of their profession, specialism, or expertise and find themselves right on the outer rim of one of the outer circles.

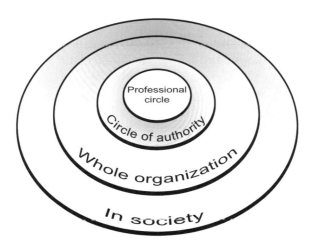

There are many examples of this inner circle: accountancy, academia, engineering, the law, science. Think of the challenge of getting a lawyer on the management board of a company to engage with non-legal issues in board meetings. Think of the scientist who becomes chair of a huge scientific body, never having operated outside the laboratory. Or, less potently but perhaps more frequently, the accountant who is given vast degrees of credibility because he knows the numbers. As Pam Chesters says: *"The deference with which people treat finance issues is frightening. They are hugely relieved if someone else is doing it, and don't take enough interest in the issues, which of course are an incredible window into an organization, to its structures and its values."*

Expert idiots can be very dangerous because, as Hans Reckers says, they are treated with *"the huge respect that their high degree of knowledge commands"* – while no one recognizes its limits.

Different situations, different positions

These positions are worth thinking about. You may already be a rebel, or a transformer, or one of the "idiots" (useful or expert). You may be all of them, at different times and in different circumstances. But in the outer circles, they come up again and again. As opportunities, as invitations, and as traps. And it's well worth knowing how to recognize them – and escape them.

What do rebels achieve and how important are they? Is change brought about best from within? Are transformers right about rebels not creating real change? Are rebels right that transformers have sold out? How do you avoid becoming a useful idiot? Are you really a useful idiot or are you really playing a very clever long game?

Maybe some of the answers lie in the combinations of the positions. Do transformers need rebels to cause the noise so that the transformers can then go on and deliver the change? Or are they deluding themselves? Are rebels right when they say that transformers just compromise and water things down? Are transformers right to claim that rebels are just angry and have limited impact?

All the positions, different times

Maybe we all play in all the positions, at different times and in different circumstances. I am a rebel on one board I sit on where I know we are getting lazy and not thinking big enough or listening hard enough, and there are no other rebels at the table. And I have become a useful idiot in another role and know full well that I need to stand up or move on. I am a transformer at Common Purpose, forging the connections across the vertical structure and making things happen. Maybe this combining is the best option. Because, for me, the worst of all worlds (bar becoming a useful idiot – without knowing it) is always being "the rebel" or "the transformer" and never breaking out of the stereotypes.

Think it through

Let's walk though this maze, in the knowledge that there are no simple answers but that the questions may be useful in themselves. Then you can decide what position – or positions – you want to play.

❑ Could you have started as a rebel and, over the years, evolved into a transformer? You started with demonstrations in the street and demands for change, and now you are working from within to bring them about.

❑ Have you gone through both rebel and transformer and are now in danger of becoming a useful idiot? You've gone from the street to the inside – and now you find that you are no longer driving the agenda, but someone else is driving yours.

❑ Maybe you have learnt the hard way and have now made sure that you are not an expert idiot. (I think of the research chemist I met recently who said: *"I could baffle you with science but I choose not to."*)

❑ Maybe you appear to be a useful idiot but, in fact, you are in it for the long game and, in time, you will steer things back on course.

❑ Perhaps you started as a transformer and now you are considering becoming a rebel? Recently, I sat with Peter Sherratt in his office at the top of a tower in Canary Wharf, looking out at the amazing view towards London from the east. Peter is Managing Director at Lehman Brothers and Chair of Governors of Oaklands School. He also runs his own private foundation to support women's education in Africa. As a lifelong transformer (and an extraordinarily successful one) he mused about whether his foundation would produce enough change by going about things gradually. And that maybe more rebellion was called for.

Dame Jane Campbell is an independent social policy adviser at the

Department of Health and former Chair of the Social Care Institute for Excellence. She has also been in a wheelchair for most of her life. She tries to balance her different roles carefully. She started as a rebel and she knows she has to be careful about becoming a useful idiot: *"I was a rebel, an angry rebel, demanding an end to my exclusion from society. I was a separatist. I would only work, and socialize with disabled people. Everyone else was the enemy. As I matured, I realized that separatism doesn't work; that we live in an integrated society, and I wanted to be part of that. I wanted to help create an ever more inclusive community where everybody could participate equally. I realized we couldn't have it both ways. When the oppressed become the oppressors, they are just as bad. I realized what a little bitch I was. I was angry and using it in an unproductive way. I had to understand my anger and move on to behaving more positively and productively. I had to move the line of tolerance and compromise. But if you move it too far then you risk becoming 'a useful idiot.' My line or set of non-negotiables has now settled. I won't get involved in anything that is not committed to the inclusion and emancipation of disabled people. For example, disability organizations and services must allow their client group to participate in their policy and strategic direction. A few years ago, I nearly got bought with promises of treasure and influence; I nearly crossed the line. What prevented me was listening to my inner voice, that instinctive judgment one acquires with experience and personal capability. Also, I had friends and a partner, who really made me think hard about what I was trying to achieve. You only really hear the people you trust."*

Rebel to transformer

What makes someone go from a rebel to a transformer? Doug Miller knows: *"You should have seen me in those days, post Vietnam. You would not have recognized me. I was a long-haired hippy. I realized fast that I had to get inside to change things. I had to get around the table."* Doug is not the only one who speaks like this. Narayana Murthy says: *"I came back from France in the mid-1970s and was converting myself from being a strong socialist, a left of center person, to what I would call a compassionate capitalist – a capitalist in mind and a liberal at heart, certainly in social matters. I wanted to create wealth legally and ethically, to run a business honestly, creating large-scale employment for people who would then have good disposable incomes. Of course, most people told me it was not possible. Indeed, it seemed so at the time."*

Seamus McAleavey is Chief Executive of the Northern Ireland Council for Voluntary Action. He makes a distinction gained, no doubt, from deep knowledge of the province: *"There are two types of rebels. There are railers, who have a vision for something different and, if they succeed as rebels, they can then make the transition to transformer. And then there are the rebels who stay 'against'; they are against, writ large. They are angry and will remain angry. Ultimately, I think people tire of the second group."*

Kuben Naidoo is Head of Fiscal Policy at the South African Treasury. His great-grandfather (when he was close to Gandhi in the 1890s), then his grandfather, followed by his father and then he himself all spent many months in prison. Rebellion runs deep in his veins: *"Moving to the Treasury was a transition from rebel to transformer – but my agenda was the same. In some ways though, it was easier to destroy apartheid than to create an equal and prosperous society. There was romance in the struggle against apartheid, in the marching and throwing stones. Now we have to change 300 years of history."* But he counters this with: *" I speak to a friend who has always been a rebel and ask him why he does not join the public sector to build the future. His response is that, if everyone did, then who would hold the public sector to account and demand that it is good? Not everyone can be co-opted into the running of the country. In civil society, you need some outside."*

So not all rebels become transformers. And, as Kuben says, it isn't easy when you do: *"You can't just rubbish the past and create a new world. Karl Marx said that a new organism had to come from within the dying one. That inherently in the old, bad one were the seeds of the good new one. That change is not a replacement of the old, but finding the good in the past and bringing it out."*

In South Africa the path from rebel to transformer is now well trodden. Cyril Ramaphosa, who is Chair of the Constitutional Assembly of South Africa, also recalls it: *"There was no real choice but to be a rebel. And, if you were, there was nothing much to lose. I do miss those days. I miss working alongside ordinary people. Meeting every night, talking and talking and persuading and getting home at three or four in the morning. But, as things changed, you had to become a transformer – because as a rebel there was no longer a power base behind you. People want you to lead the transformation. Rebels who won't adapt start to lose their relevance and become empty vessels. But, once you become a transformer, the rebel in you still has to keep pushing for faster and deeper change."*

Rebels and transformers need each other

Peter Tatchell says he learnt a lot from the early campaigns for voting rights for women: *"Think of the suffragists and the suffragettes. The former group worked inside the system, while the latter assailed it from the outside. The suffragists campaigned slowly over time to win votes for women, lobbying the establishment using facts and arguments. The suffragettes decided that the softly-softly approach was not working. Their suffragist sisters were often patronized or ignored. To break this logjam, the suffragettes used direct action protest as a way of pushing women's votes into the headlines, generating public awareness and debate, and putting the political elite on the spot. Their militancy eventually helped push the establishment into negotiating with the suffragists. The efforts of both groups reinforced each other, though most of their members would not have recognized this. In fact, they both frequently denounced each other. But, to secure the franchise for women, you needed both the insiders and outsiders; the transformers and the rebels."* The arch-rebel knows full well how much he needs transformers to complete the work he starts: *"You need to keep reminding yourself that a protest is a means to an end, not an end in itself."*

Doug Miller, ever the transformer, agrees: *"We need the radicals on the outside to force the issues onto the agenda, and then the insiders can maneuver them through. The radical rebels would say they could achieve more without the compromisers – but they would be wrong. You need people chipping away from the inside too."*

Avoiding the useful idiot position

If the greatest thing potential useful idiots have to offer is their personal brand, then maybe this is what you have to protect the most. Seamus McAleavey and I talk about celebrities who might have come close to handing over their brand to someone else. They are perhaps the most vulnerable because, in modern days, their brands are the most sought after. Maybe Sir Bob Geldof, that brave man who has stood up and been counted so often, has come closer to it than many. Or one might consider Bono. Seamus observes that: *"Bono has been more clever than many celebrities. He has assessed the new territory, figured out the game. He has listened, and taken it all in. He won't settle for any win. He has become more self-deprecating, because you have to be in touch with ordinary people and be seen to be. You have to show you are grounded, otherwise people think you are in it for yourself. People need to trust you and, if they think there is something else going on, they won't."*

Roisín McDonough has a personal brand that radiates commitment and balance and charm and decency, built up over years in Northern Ireland. She warns about the useful idiot role: *"If you know that nothing is going on and you are only sought to adorn some venture and add your own credibility to it, be careful. Even worse, don't do it if the new venture is only being undertaken as a way to prevent something better from emerging. Ask yourself: are you just there as window dressing?"* It is a very difficult call. Hans Reckers talks about this dilemma: *"In East Germany, as it was, you had a choice: to leave and walk away, which many did; to stay and not to participate in the political system; or to stay and try to influence things. If you chose the last, you ran the risk of becoming a useful idiot, and then you would achieve nothing."*

Cyril Ramaphosa shares Roisín's view on the risk – but he developed a fairly extreme way of avoiding it: *"There was always the risk that I would become a useful idiot. Just when it might have happened, I would get arrested again and I became less useful."*

How do you spot when useful idiocy is being thrust upon you? It can be quite beguiling and gradual. Emma, my 17-year-old daughter, challenged a friend who came for Saturday lunch recently. He had just been appointed to the House of Lords as a new independent peer. He is black and Emma asked him: *"Do you ever worry that you were appointed to fill a quota?"* He roared with laughter and replied: *"Of course."* But that he was not going to miss the opportunity because of it. I shall watch my friend and try to help spot the traps. The early symptoms will be if he starts phoning people to make sure they have his title properly on their lists. Or if he begins to invite people for "tea" on the "terrace" at the "House" (a beautiful space, especially in the summer, looking up at Westminster Bridge) to discuss how incredibly important the work of the House is. The worst will be if he starts to adorn committees addressing issues he knows absolutely nothing about. Knowing him, I suspect he will be a wonderful contributor to the House of Lords, which occasionally addresses issues that others would prefer to bury and gets our government to think again. But he will need help, as we all would. Because flattery and flak will be coming his way for sure.

Useful – but not such an idiot

A word of caution from Deirdre Hutton: *"Let's not write off useful idiots too quickly. Sometimes, you might think they are and in fact they are just playing the long game. When all the others have fallen away, they will pull it off."* Also, don't let the fear of becoming a useful idiot put you off leaving the core circle.

I have a good friend who has become a major transformer in Northern Ireland. He describes what happens when rebels turn transformer there: *"There's an expression here which is used to discredit Roman Catholics who seek to effect change from inside the system. We're called Castle Catholics."* (The "castle" is Stormont, the center of power in Northern Ireland). Almost all cultures have horrible expressions for people they claim have turned away from what are perceived to be their roots. The words are invariably hard and hurtful – and designed to force "traitors" to go back into their core circle (or never consider leaving it). *"I know some people think I am becoming a 'Castle Catholic.' It's a bit like 'useful idiot.' It's also one of the oldest dilemmas. My response is, 'I know it's a dirty game – but it's the only game in town.' You have to be part of things. If you stay on the outside, you surrender your influence. To friends who stay in their core circle, I say: 'OK, so you remained uncontaminated and pure – so what?' But, if you are going to move to the outer circles, you have to stay very close to people who will tell you when you are going too far. You have to build in your own compromises; and keep a sharp eye on the limits of your own impact, so that you don't start to kid yourself it's worth staying around when it isn't any more."*

SCENARIO: PROMISED LAND OR POISONED CHALICE?

You have been asked by the government to lead an inquiry into a mess up. You are a well-respected leader and have experience of working with government. It is complex, high profile, and involves elected representatives and appointed officials in two separate government departments. Should you take it on?"

Sir Michael Bichard is Rector of the University of the Arts in London and former Permanent Secretary at the Department of Education. He also chaired the Soham Inquiry.

It's always flattering to be asked, but stop and think – very carefully. Am I likely to have the skills to do this? Will I be acceptable to the people most closely involved? Could I possibly be perceived to have any kind of interest or bias? Are the politicians from all sides going to co-operate with me and trust me? Is it sufficiently important to justify what will be a huge amount of time – and can I make the time available? Am I physically and emotionally up to this at the moment? Do I think I can get the necessary support team in place quickly? Can I ensure that I will have the freedom to report honestly and objectively, whatever needs to be said? Will the media welcome my appointment? Is my current office support able to cope with the pressure and the subject?

If the answer to those questions is mostly positive, take a deep breath and agree. Then get the team in place as quickly as you possibly can and find somewhere to base the office; read yourself into the subject very fast so that you look and sound competent from the outset; work with the media and give them the best service (including technology) you can muster.

Realize that everyone is under stress and treat everyone with respect. Don't jump to conclusions. Don't appoint anyone to the team who you think can't handle people sensitively – or who lacks commitment. Never ever give anyone reason to doubt your fairness and integrity.

Janet Paraskeva is the First Commissioner at the Civil Service Commission and former Chief Executive of the Law Society.

I would do my own due diligence – but I would not wait until I knew all the facts first. I think that if you really knew what you were letting yourself in for, you probably wouldn't do anything.

I need to know enough so that I know if I am excited by it, and if there is a real job to be done that I can do.

Sir Derek Higgs is Chair of Alliance and Leicester plc. He chaired the Independent Review of Non-Executive Directors.

Before I took it on, I'd establish:

❑ who my client is (to avoid the crossfire of a departmental tug of war)
❑ whether this is a "hospital pass" (as in too many government enquiries where the hapless individual is there to dispense whitewash, and as a result suffers public pillorying)
❑ whether I will be paid (a no-win situation: if you are paid, you're not wholly independent; if you're not paid, what are you doing it for?)
❑ how long it will take (multiply any estimate supplied in advance by three)
❑ whether I can cope with the media (it can get very wearing)
❑ And finally, if am I the right person to do this (i.e., was I first or twenty-first on the list of candidates for the role)?

Geoff Mulgan is Director of the Young Foundation and former Head of Policy at No.10 Downing Street.

Usually, when someone's asked to head up an inquiry, it means that something has gone badly wrong. The world needs to know what happened, who to blame – and what can be done differently. You're asked because you're seen as independent, wise, and good at getting to the bottom of things. The first response many people have in such situations is to feel flattered. It's nice to be seen as the answer to something; it's reassuring to be seen as useful. But that's also the moment to be most rigorous in asking yourself whether you can really do it.

So I would go carefully.

The first thing I would do is examine the brief. Presumably, I have been asked because neither civil servants nor ministers feel up to tackling it – or at least, anything they do is unlikely to be legitimate. So one question I would need to think about is whether there is likely to be a viable way through and, just as important, whether there is an appetite for finding it. This is where terms of reference are all-important. For example, if I am asked to sort out the pensions crisis (as Adair Turner was) but I'm not allowed to look at state pensions, I should be worried. If I am asked to look at just one slice of a problem and not the whole picture, my job may be impossible or, at least, flawed from the start (as in the case of Hutton). Equally, I would be worried if there were profound differences between the interests involved, since I am bound to get caught in the crossfire.

Then there are more basic questions. Will I have the resources needed to do the job? Will I have access to the data I need? Will I get support if there are tough conclusions?

Perhaps the hardest questions are the ones I have to ask about myself. Do I have the guile? Am I streetwise enough to navigate a really messy public situation? This is very hard for people whose main background is business. If the going gets tough, do I know how to use the media and communicate to the public to outflank my enemies? This is equally hard for people brought up on management consultancy and PowerPoint. Do I have the intellectual capacities – and the humility – to deal with a complex situation? I must have heard dozens of business leaders who genuinely believed that they could sort out the NHS, given half a chance. The small minority who really got to know about health ended up a lot more humble. Above all, do I have the appetite to make enemies? Because, if I do my job well, I may well upset people.

We have to hope that enough people can answer all these questions positively – because it is a great asset for public life to have genuinely independent people asking difficult questions and coming up with challenging answers. Just don't expect everyone to love you for it.

Sue Stapely is a solicitor and reputation management consultant at Quiller Consultants.

Poisoned chalices rarely appeal – and few public enquiries give rise to plaudits or career enhancement for those who lead them. I need to ask myself:

❑ How serious are the problems which have given rise to the mess? There's a big difference between yet another silly man with zipper trouble and real financial impropriety.
❑ And how do I really feel about the issues themselves? Am I

supportive of the Government and the Ministers responsible for the departments under scrutiny? Will my cynicism about much of modern political life be thought to color my objectivity?

The considerations are personal and professional – they often blur. I would need to be clear why *I* had been asked to tackle this task. Do they want a rigorous scrutiny by an objective outsider, with the findings presented robustly? Is there acceptance of the possibility of political embarrassment if errors, oversights or worse are identified? Or do they want a cursory examination of the issues, giving rise to an anodyne report which could be discreetly buried? Am I being asked because a woman with advancing arthritis ticks a few of the diversity boxes, or is thought to be more of a pushover than a man? Just how did they get my name?

If I accept this challenge, will I be able to manage expectations and deliver work of which I can be proud? Have I the time, will I receive the support and resources I need, and will my advice and opinions be heeded on how the process should be managed? Who will be the secretary to the inquiry and the others with whom I will have to liaise – and can I work cordially and constructively with them? In other words, how much control and influence will I really have? Many people who have undertaken work of this sort have complained that they are given unrealistic timelines, provided with minimal staffing, and either stuck with writing the report unsupported or presented with someone else's prose and have to battle to put their own stamp on it.

Will I be free to present the findings myself and manage their communication? As someone who works professionally in this field, how difficult will I find it to be constrained by others? How will this matter play in the media and how much can I influence its handling?

Are the two departments involved in competition with each other for the same political turf – or keen to finger the other for responsibility for whatever problems have arisen? Are the Ministers and officials supportive of an inquiry, or intent on blocking its progress and burying its findings?

Am I comfortable with the personal exposure? Will people Google my name as soon as my appointment is announced and challenge my suitability? Will my support of the Legalise Cannabis campaign from the 1960s come back to haunt me again? Will my unsuccessful attempts to become an MP be derided? And the fact that I marched against the war in Iraq? Will my day job as a lawyer and reputation management consultant be construed as a sign that I have been asked to spin this issue into oblivion? Will my future career be jeopardized by accepting this position or by the coverage it attracts?

Working systematically through these questions and more should lead me to my answer. Unless I am confident that I can deliver a professional piece of work which will withstand public scrutiny, answer all legitimate questions, and lead to meaningful changes to improve things, I should decline the opportunity to fail – and to fail publicly.

PART 6

What does it take?

The ability to cross worlds

Leaders today must be able to operate in a multitude of overlapping worlds: racial, cultural, political, geographical, religious, and social. It is no longer possible to succeed by concentrating on one of these worlds and ignoring the rest. Tom Cummings talks about needing *"the ability to cross worlds."* He believes that there are various stages for a leader: *"The first is expressed as 'I live in a world, that's it. It's the only one for me and I'm doing well in it.' The second is, 'There is my world, but I can also see lots of other worlds and compare them to mine. But I am clear that I prefer to stick to mine.' The next one, 'Sometimes I venture into other worlds, and I enjoy it, but I still always revert,' sometimes moves on to 'I operate in lots of worlds but I can't yet figure out how to connect them.' And then, if you go the whole way, 'I live in multiple worlds, and have the capacity to integrate them all.'"* Across organizations and in society we need many, many more leaders who get to Tom's ultimate stage.

When leaders attend Common Purpose programs, I know we can get them all to the penultimate stage but, in truth, we don't get them all the whole way. Both are worth achieving – and it is inspiring when you watch their triumphs. People often ask me to "prove" the Common Purpose effect. They want a list of outcomes claimed, projects started, and new initiatives completed. I know we have to spend time satisfying them, but what I love is helping to develop leaders who operate across worlds. Who counteract the forces of fragmentation in organizations and society. Who – together – make two and two make eight (or even ten). If you believe in leadership, if you know that *"fish rot from the head"* and that if you don't get the leaders right then everything falls apart, that is enough.

Different skills

Before he retired, Sir Brandon Gough was Senior Partner of Coopers & Lybrand, first in the UK and then globally. He was also the second

Chair of the Common Purpose trustees. He was extraordinary to watch as a leader beyond his authority. You have to be if you lead a partnership – especially a partnership of accountants. He had a way at meetings, even when you could see that everyone was going in every possible direction, with each person seeing different things and taking different positions, and when there was no great need to agree – and certainly no need to please Brandon. When it came to the summarizing of the points, he would launch off and, before you knew it, everyone in the room was nodding. It was an extraordinary skill. I went to see him to get him to share his secrets. Having spent most of his professional life beyond his authority, he took most of them as self-evident. So it took some time and pushing, but what I really wanted to know was how did he learn the skills? He talked about his early career: *"I was given the job of leading a group charged with producing a new audit method to be used right across our organization internationally. This was an important strategic initiative, but the exercise had become bogged down and my job was to sort it out. There were two challenges. The first was technical: formidable but capable of being overcome. The second, and bigger, challenge arose from differences in attitude among the working party members and the national businesses they represented. As leader of a group which was expected to operate by consensus, I was at a disadvantage in two respects: I didn't have executive powers and I was less experienced than most of my new colleagues.*

I started by analyzing the situation, looking at it as a whole, and then identifying areas of agreement and disagreement. By breaking it down into bits, I could start to make progress. What I gradually learnt served me well later when I became the senior partner and also when I moved outside my firm into other activities.

First, and this was intuitive, don't accept that there is a real difference in position until it can be demonstrated. You need to look for the substance in an issue that appears to divide people. Remember that one of the problems with meetings is that they can exaggerate apparent differences. Sometimes it's because participants feel they have to be brief, so they oversimplify their point, or they don't say everything that is on their mind. Often, the difference in positions is nothing like as great as it would appear. Of course, you need to understand the strength of opinions in a room, but you need to be careful not to overstate them, or become dominated by them.

Second, you need to make progress meeting by meeting, creating momentum, never losing ground. In that way, you build authority.

You have to be prepared to play a long game but always be ready to grab an opportunity to accelerate if it arises.

Third, you have to build personal coalitions; decide where to form links and when to isolate people who are blockers. How do you isolate people who are stopping progress? First intellectually, showing that they are not on strong ground, that their point is not worth making, or that their argument is not compelling. Second you have to persuade other people to stand up to the blocker, to show that the price is not high, or that the blocker and allies will back off if resisted.

So there is a requirement for both hard and soft skills: the hard skills of analysis and solution development, and the soft skills of managing personalities and relationships. It's worth remembering that the hard skills can get you so far, but often not to a desirable conclusion."

Does age help?

You hear a lot about the wisdom that comes with age. I have a feeling that wisdom is a bit of an illusion – one of those words designed to make you feel better about getting old. I am not sure that age is helpful. We all need the ability to make mistakes and learn from them and accumulate that learning, but this is not necessarily connected with age. I think resilience, good health, and stamina are worth more.

Does being a woman help?

Some people ask me if women are better at leading beyond authority than men. I am sure there is some truth in this, but I am not sure it's about being a woman, per se. I reject the developing expression "female leadership." I have seen far too many men, including Brandon Gough, who know it's not just about hard stuff to believe in "female" leadership skills.

There is something here though. As Roisín McDonough says from her experience of Belfast, which is so rich in hugely powerful and impressive women who are not at the top of organizations: *"It is because women have been kept out of many positions of power. They have got better at leading beyond authority and working on the margins. They have learnt to create power."* Sue Stapely agrees: *"Women have more experience of negotiating comfort zones. They may not have worked their way up through authority. They are also often more attuned to the need to adjust."* Maybe Darwin was really talking about women when he said: *"It's not the strongest of the species that survives, nor the most intelligent. It is the one that is most adaptable to change.*" Bharat Mehta runs the City Parochial Foundation, which funds community activities all over London. He has backed and watched successful social entrepreneurs, male and female, for years: "*Community activists tend to be very effective in the outer circle because they have never had authority. They don't yearn for it and dream of the speed at which things can go when they had it.*" Thinking of people who run partnerships – Brandon Gough, Diana Parker, Janet Gaymer, Bill Knight – I wonder if people are better at leading outside the core circle if they've had less authority than most within it. Perhaps Darwin was talking about women, community activists, and leaders of partnerships.

Does parenting help?

A friend often tells me that it helps if you're a parent: "*They never ask a child what they want for tea, so as to elicit a long list of things that are not in the house. They launch instead into real excitement about what there is for tea, none of which the child will be able to resist.*" Jane Earl is the Director of the Assets Recovery Agency. She thinks along the same lines: " *Motherhood of teenagers for me has been a real learning ground for leading beyond authority. You learn low cunning. You learn to find every sort of answer to the question 'This affects me how?' You get better and better at formulating sentences that start with 'What's in it for you is ...' Sometimes it's the only way to get teenagers out of bed.*"

Learning from the best

Alison Coburn develops Common Purpose internationally. Eight years ago, she packed her bags and got on a plane to South Africa. At the time, we had three programs operating outside the UK: Dublin in Ireland, Orebro in Sweden, and Hannover in Germany. She walked around Johannesburg, speaking to anyone who would talk to her. She even persuaded Cyril Ramaphosa, a businessman and the Chairman of the Constitutional Assembly of South Africa, to back Common Purpose. Why did he do it? Because, as he says: "*We cannot wait for great ideas from great people to solve democracy's problems. We must look to each other. Every one of us has the power to transform our own lives and the lives of people around us. That is what democracy means.*"

Since then, Alison has started Common Purpose in Frankfurt,

Leipzig, Hamburg, Amsterdam, and Budapest. More will follow soon (in recent weeks, she has returned from successful exploratory trips to Istanbul and Bangalore).

In her travels, Alison "lives" leading beyond her authority and has met some of the best. When I was first thinking about undertaking this book, she and I sat and wrote down what it is about people who lead beyond authority that makes us feel good as we walk out of their offices after the first meeting. We came up with three common factors: the right approach, the love of people, and never to be under-estimated, the right method.

Their approach gives us confidence that they won't disappear when it gets tough. They will adapt their leadership to the situation. It's not about them – they will go wherever they can be most effective. They will lead from the front, the middle, the side, or the back. They will see the vision and be able to express it so that it resonates. They are independent, in every sense of the word.

Because they love people, they make you feel bigger, taller, than when you went in. They have huge networks that they are happy to use. Their assumptions are constantly under review, and they adapt to any situation, so you don't feel you have been judged (even if you have).

They have the right method, they are tactically astute. They know how things work in different worlds and they don't underestimate the differences. They will take time to think things through and get things right. They know how to set a pace and how to build coalitions. Being around them will be fun and exciting. And things will happen when you leave their office.

Leaders who master the three sets of skills that Alison and I identi-fied are the ones who legitimize themselves. And, as they do, people simply stop questioning their right to be operating in the outer circles.

THE RIGHT APPROACH 1: COURAGE

Into the unknown

You cannot launch yourself into the unknown without courage. Think of the great explorers. They used to set off from Europe in their ships and, as they got further out, the terrible moment came nearer when they could no longer see the land, yet they could not yet read the night stars. It must have been horrifying. And what if you thought that the world was flat and that you would eventually be falling off the side? It took an extraordinary degree of courage. Leaving behind most of what you knew and understood and had mastered. There may well have been great mariners on the ship who far preferred the sea. There may also have been people who had done it before and knew it was OK. They needed to be generous to the sailor in fear and share their knowledge. I think the same happens when you leave your core circle for the outer ones. There must come a moment when you realize that you can't just turn around and go back. We certainly need those who have done it before to share their knowledge.

Check your instincts

All leaders need to be brave if anyone is going to follow them, either in or beyond their authority. But they also need to be sensible. A couple of years ago, on holiday, a friend went out with her daughter in a small sailing boat. It got choppy and they overturned. My friend was not a strong swimmer and she was in quite a mess. My husband and I set out to save her in our bigger boat. As we approached, I jumped into the water, with only her and the need to help her in mind. Of course, it was the last thing I should have done. I did comfort her – but now I could no longer save her and there were two people in the water. I have never lived it down. Yes it was brave – but stupid too! Then, only a week or so later, we went out sailing as a family. I have never claimed to be a sailor, but the joys of motherhood require me to join in. The sea got pretty rough and my husband shouted for me to do something about Tom, who was five and entirely happily sitting at the back, enjoying the rough ride and waves. So I worked my way to the back and tied a rope around him so that we could get him back on board if he did go overboard. When we finally hit dry land, my husband suggested that it would have been better not to tie him to the anchor rope. The sea and sailing, I know nothing of them and all my instincts fail me. This is not safe territory for me. I don't lack courage

– but I do the wrong thing almost every time. Everything I know on dry land is wrong at sea. It is so frightening when the instincts that you rely upon are misleading and when your reasoning powers fail you because you are so very far out.

You need sensible courage in the outer circles. So as not to go back – especially when everything you know fails to match the situation. And even more when you have messed up on something. Janet Paraskeva says: *"Some people think of me as fearless, but I'm not. It is just that I am not frightened of the same things. In fact, lots of things frighten me, particularly the dark when I can't see where I am going and what's coming at me."*

Coping with the vitriol

You need courage to cope with the vitriol in the outer circles. Of course, none of us become leaders – in or beyond authority – because we are looking for a round of applause; there never will be one for most of us. But, in the outer circles, it can be pretty unpleasant when people want you out of their way. As Deirdre Hutton says: *"There may be strong voices ranged against you."* Maybe they just don't want to change, or they don't want what they perceive to be inappropriate scrutiny. They will challenge your legitimacy and use all kinds of ways – maybe even personal – to shut you up so that they can get on with their comfortable lives. John Inge agrees: *"You have to learn to cope with vitriol. Sometimes, of course, you simply have to confront it sharply. A generally better technique is to attempt to soak it up, because taking it on can so often perpetuate the vicious circle. Turning the other cheek has got itself a bad name: too many equate it with being a doormat. But to turn the other cheek is to rob the oppressor of control. It's to say: 'You want to slap me on the cheek? I don't care. Slap me on the other as well.' Gandhi and Mandela have proved the extraordinary power of this approach in the political sphere."*

Keeping going

Courage sometimes means resilience: the courage to keep going and never accept no. As James Ramsbotham says: *"If you look at the three circles carefully, you discover that they are actually spinning – and spinning in a way that will spin you back into the core. So you have to swim even harder and with great courage to get out. And if you tread water you slide back."* You have to cope with the complexity, without attempting to simplify it. I sometimes wonder if our fear of complexity is almost debilitating these days. As my former Chef de Cabinet said to me: *"In the past, we wanted to explore and conquer complexity. Now we just want it to go away."* Sometimes, you know full well it would be easier to give up. Then you won't have to keep on mustering the courage.

Feedback: giving and taking

Then there is the courage to accept and give feedback. To many, it is almost impossible either to hear from others what they think, and to deal with it (whether right or wrong), or to give feedback when you know it is likely to upset people. The British must surely be the worst at this? They store it all up and it comes out in a gush when they can't hold it in any longer. But then, it's no longer courage, it's confession – and it's usually horrible. Baroness Margaret Ford, says that the best leaders beyond their authority: *"are brave enough to cope with feedback. If you get feedback, then you learn to listen, and you listen more, and to more people. Too many of us don't get feedback and can't take it without taking our bats and balls home."* But giving it is hard too. Leaders go to huge trouble to avoid giving feedback, because it's difficult and embarrassing and often personal, and it's easy to get it wrong. Ask Stranger Two: *"You have to learn the skills of constructive challenge; of challenging people in a way that they know you are trying to help, and not trying to belittle them. If you are not very careful, as you challenge, you stop people in their tracks. Even worse, you start telling people what to do. And though this is possible within your authority, if you are beyond it, then you get lost. In giving feedback your aim is not to stop people, but to get them to think again."*

Exercise the muscle

You do need to know what to exercise your courage on. As Deirdre Hutton says: *"Weak people often make stands on the wrong things."* Maybe they have given way and given way and suddenly they say *"I'm not going to be pushed around any longer"* and they dig their heels in without considering whether this is the right thing to make a stand on. Deirdre says you need to know when to give way. She must have been watching me in the sea, because she also says: *"There are very few situations where blind courage is appropriate. Rather you need cool, rational courage, and this goes with persistence and resilience."*

Baroness May Blood is a community worker in Shankill Road in Belfast. She knows about bravery. She says that courage is like any muscle: *"if you don't exercise it enough, it becomes weak and unreliable."* Most leaders need to remember this. Moving out of their core circle and beyond their authority will help to keep it exercised.

THE RIGHT APPROACH 2:
HUMILITY AND SELF-BELIEF

Chris Mathias says: *"Ten years ago, the words I associated with leadership were: focus, clarity, integrity, determination, and unwavering. I would never have put humility on the list; it was never part of the mental model. I have now discovered that it is far more powerful to lead with humility. It's about the ability to lead from the inside and not just from the head."*

Every single person I have ever spoken to about leading beyond authority has used the word humility in their first breath. This is irrespective of the country or continent they came from, the background they grew up in, or the roles beyond authority that they have held. Many have expressed surprise, like Chris, about the rude awakening to its importance – and to the realization of their own unimportance. My father used to talk about Henry Ford, who apparently was wandering around a boardroom mid-meeting, getting bad tempered, and looked out of the window. He saw a graveyard and muttered: *"Look – full of essential people."* You need a sharp sense of your own importance, or lack of it. My father also had a wonderful north of England expression for a certain type of person whom he did not much take to: *"He's a self-made man who is proud of his maker."* Such leaders don't do well outside the core circle and without recourse to authority. Andrew Cubie is Chair of Napier University in Edinburgh. He talks about having the confidence *"to keep causing ripples and hope that some will turn into waves. What is important is how high the water reaches on distant shores."*

This is very different from the thrusting approach to leadership, what I like to think of as the "fourteenth-century knights" attitude: all about being focused, determined, and unwavering, the "loneliness of command," and all that. There is no doubt that, for many, this is very effective in the core circle. But, whether it's your style or not, it won't work in the outer circles. And I'd go further: I believe it won't deliver for very much longer in the core circle either. Because people will deliver OK if authority requires them to but, if they are to deliver of their very best, they need more. They need vision and a sense of involvement. And without them, both people and organizations can perish very quickly.

What made Chris change his mind about humility? Meeting a man called Naidoo, who runs an organization called Basic Needs India:

"I spent nine days traveling with Naidoo. His passion is to work with the disenfranchised and the marginalized in Indian society – people

with no voice and no options. And in India it is hard to find anyone more marginalized than the mentally ill. In the villages of India, views on mental illness are archaic – and the cures even more so. Evil spirits are driven out by beating, outbursts controlled by chaining the person constantly, families hide mentally ill relatives – because bad blood runs in the family, and so on. And there is no natural constituency on which you can rely when you're working with these people. Naidoo can only lead beyond his authority because – in the highly structured society that is India – he has no authority by birth, and none by his status. He travels from village to village with his entire worldly possessions in his bag, and it is a small one, about the half the size of my carry-on luggage for a plane. He wonders why anyone (and me specifically) would want any more than that. Wherever he goes, people gather around and he talks about mental illness and, through his quiet conversations and calm presence, he persuades people to think differently – and to change mindsets that have been held for generations. He sometimes takes a small group of actors whom he has trained to act out plays in the village center. That too is great for gathering the villagers – and the messages work. In time, families will bring out their 'hidden' relatives and the large local NGOs will start to show an interest. It is through working with the local NGOs that Naidoo and Basic Needs India have achieved such huge impact. As a result of that journey, I completely changed my ideas of leadership. It is not about all the 'crunchy' values. It is much more about humility, belief, commitment, persuasion, and selflessness."

Elizabeth Dow is President of Leadership Philadelphia. She says that humility is a recurring theme on the Community Leadership programs in the USA (which are not unlike Common Purpose programs in the UK): *"I met a woman in Philadelphia who was a welfare mother with seven kids, living on $5,000 a year. Her leadership spirit had led her to create a non-profit [organization] that helped women move from welfare to work. I asked her if she wanted to come on the program. Her answer was that she did not have a Master's degree. On the program, she teamed up with a smart guy with a law degree from Harvard. She learnt that she could hold her own with him. He saw her talent and will never think of women on welfare in the same way. It was humbling for him – and empowering for her."*

Observing leaders, I think those who can best lead beyond authority are the ones who replace authority with self-belief. And it is self-belief rather than simply confidence. Maybe the very best even throw away what little authority they have when they are in the outer circles, because it can get in the way. I increasingly believe that the combination of humility and self-belief, the careful balancing of the two, is what is so potent and allows them to operate without a shred of authority.

What can knock the humility out of you?

Worries about being found out, revealed as a fool, a fraud, or a failure. These haunt you. Then remember the flattery and the flak. Seeing your name in newspapers sometimes makes fools of even the best of us, tempting us to believe what is written there, good or bad. Derek Higgs says: *"Be careful if you start to believe all the rubbish written about you. The further you go out, and up, the greater the risk that your feet start to lift off the ground."* Sir Michael Bichard comments: *" Once you go out of your circle, the pull to go further out gets stronger and stronger. As you succeed, your view is sought on ever greater issues, and this is when you need to get really careful – careful what you get involved in. The danger is that you start to become a useful idiot, because you lose the humility and start to pronounce on issues on which you know nothing or next to nothing and where you have no useful contribution to make. In fact, you may even cause damage. Of course, you need to do things that push you, make you think, use your contacts. But don't become so arrogant that you think you can talk about anything."* Amy Fawcett and Doug Miller have the same view. From Amy: *"One potential danger in the outer circle in the UK today is the significant deference that is given to leaders from the private sector. You are given a fairly significant voice, which is good at one level, but can be damaging if it is not tempered as and when appropriate."* And Doug: *"Beware the respect that comes your way."* If you lose the humility, I think your days are numbered beyond your authority (maybe inside too, but it takes longer). I am thinking about a major leader in the UK, who ran an enormous PLC and chaired a number of very exciting initiatives for the government. Why did he come unstuck? I suspect it was mostly about him. He became arrogant about his knowledge in the outer circles and, later, his status too. He stopped being prepared to concede. He surrounded himself with people who admired him. He did not have an un-pompous partner at home who could at least keep his feet on the ground in the evenings and at weekends. And he had too much to prove to people, especially previous bosses, who had not backed him over the years.

Learning from the best

If you start with humility, you tend to see leadership in another way. Let me explain. Every summer I spend August on an island off the west coast of Scotland. I have five children and I always seem to acquire other people's children too. We set off on a lovely day to go to a beach on the northwest side of the island called Balnahard. At about 11 o'clock, a man who was holidaying on the island and had joined our group (when he is not on holiday, he is in total charge of a big organization) came and asked me, in a rather frustrated and grumpy fashion, who was leading the expedition. Rather confused, I said that I was. He asked me therefore who was going to get to the Balnahard beach first. Even more confused, I said that I did not really care who did. He sighed. I clearly lacked drive. He then looked up at my son on the cliffs, obviously irritated. I had to admit, it was a worrying sight, but I said: *"Well, he is 20. And I don't think he will fall off that cliff. He will probably come back and rejoin us sometime soon and, for the last part of the journey, he will probably carry all the bags."* The man went off muttering about poor leadership. And I walked on muttering about people who wanted to get to the beach first. Fourteenth-century knights: people who cannot see that you do not have to be out in front to lead, with all the party lined up behind you, and the clear intention of getting to the beach first.

When I got back to work after the summer, the usual piles of post sat on my desk to be sorted. Among them were four invitations to speak at high-powered leadership conferences. They all seemed to me to be asking for variants on a theme of "how to get to the beach first." They weren't for me. There was one other invitation in the pile: asking if I would like to come and speak about "female leadership." My colleagues had – sensibly – put it in the does-not-require-speedy-answer file.

From the back

Beyond authority, I don't think you can spend too much time thinking about who is going to get to the beach first. I love that Gandhi quote: *"There go my people. I must go with them, for I am their leader."*

Great leaders beyond authority are humble, have self-belief, and don't care where they lead from. Sometimes it's from the front, because that's what is called for. Sometimes it's from the side, backing up someone else.

Sometimes it's from the middle, because only there can you sense what is needed. Sometimes it's from the back, because the momentum is there and others just need you to be somewhere. People who worry about the elitism implied by the word leadership sometimes call this "follower-ship" but, to me, it's just another kind of leadership. You could argue that, as Gandhi rushed to catch up with his people, whom he had led so well that they would set off without him, he was following them. I think it is still leadership, just coming from another angle. Full of both self-belief and humility.

From the front

When I started Common Purpose, I had no choice but to lead from the front – there was nowhere else because, at the outset, there was no one else. It was when I recruited the first group of very able, very bright colleagues that the dilemma of how to lead them first came to the surface. I felt slightly in awe of them. I felt that my job now was to support them as they charged ahead. So, internally at least, I chose to lead from the back. But it didn't feel right, and the longer it went on, the clearer it became that this was the wrong time (and the wrong way) to do it. Things came to a head when they told me that, in order to have legitimacy as the leader of the organization, I had to run a program myself. I knew that this would slow us down. I had to keep going to new places and starting new programs. (In 1994, I got the InterCity Rail Traveller of the Year award, because I spent an average of 23 hours a week on trains.) In the end, I went to see John Garnett, who ran the Industrial Society (where I got my first job after leaving university) to ask his advice. He was adamant: I had to stop trying to lead these people from the back, to overtake and set out ahead. Not so far that I left them behind, but far enough that they would have to run to catch up with me.

From the side

Prue Leith is a businesswoman, restaurateur, and writer. She is also a highly successful "social entrepreneur." She had been to an Open-Ground gathering at which a really interesting idea had emerged which was now gaining momentum. I visited her because I wanted to get her more deeply involved. She laughed at me. She said I was perfecting the art of leading from the side: by doing the *"donkey work."* New initiatives had emerged from OpenGround over the years but, as we know, plenty of great ideas never get off the ground because someone forgot to set up the meeting or book the room. I have certainly been the leader from the side in the fledgling days for many of these new ideas, often doing the boring, background work that no one else really fancied taking on, until the momentum built up and then others took over. I have also seen some great campaigners do the same. They put themselves at the disposal of others. They write papers and build coalitions. They volunteer their resources and expertise. As the people who are offered all this get going, they find they need this support more and more and, before you know it, no one knows who is leading whom.

John Inge agrees: *"The best clergy see where the spirit moves and follow. They go where the energy is. As a young incumbent on Tyneside, I had one thousand and one things to do but I soon learned to listen to people and to support and encourage them when they felt moved to act. Many good things resulted. Like Viv starting a lunch club for the elderly which 40 people attended each week. I think it is unhealthy if, as a leader, you are concerned predominantly with being in control. It's the child in us that makes us want to be. Good leadership is exercised by those who are secure enough in themselves to be able to relinquish control as well as exercise it responsibly."*

From the middle

There are some great examples of leading from the middle too. Lord Gordon is a non-executive director of Johnston Press and former managing director of a local radio station, Radio Clyde. He talks about the *"collie dog"* approach to leadership, which he perfected because a radio station is made up of a series of individuals who will seldom accept any form of authority. He says the aim is to get them all to go roughly in the same direction, to persuade them they are all working for themselves and just happen to be contributing to the whole in the process. He talks about *"releasing the spring in people"* that makes them want to do something more than the task that they were given. When collie dogs herd sheep, they take them roughly in one direction, but not in formation. They chase after the ones that really wander off in the wrong direction and, even then, they only nudge them back in. You can let people go out quite far, but you must keep your eye on them. Chris Mathias says this analogy doesn't work for him at all. He says it's too coherent: *"It's better to let a thousand blossoms bloom. The herding analogy also implies that the herdsman has a purposeful direction, which he often hasn't."* Chris's view is that the challenge, when you are beyond your authority, is to persuade those you are seeking to lead to have the same internal sense of direction as you, *"without them knowing or you telling them."*

So, you need courage so that you stand up, and then humility and self-belief so that people will go with you. Recently, I went to see someone who has taken on a huge leading beyond authority task, in truth to offer help. He sat there and effectively said *"Impress me."* I'll leave him to find his own way.

THE RIGHT APPROACH 3: INDEPENDENCE

Not a state – an attitude

Independence is not a role or a position. It is not about whether you have the word independent in your job title or your job description. It is about how you are. It's a state of mind. You need to be independent to operate in the outer circles – and you need to be known as independent too. "*There is a strongly held view that whoever pays the piper calls the tune,*" Andrew Cubie admits, but he goes on to point out that: "*Of course, effective leaders will always manage to retain their independence. That is one of their marks. However, even if this is true, it has also to appear to be so today – because, sadly, perception is seen by many as more important than reality.*"

James Ramsbotham agrees: "*You cannot change much if you are not considered to be legitimate, and you won't be if there is any evidence or perception that you are in it for yourself. Because, let's face it, there are an awful lot of people scrutinizing you in the outer circles.*"

Some months ago, I read an article about a local politician who had resigned from the planning committee. In a subsequent interview with a local newspaper, he explained that he simply could not overcome his deep hatred of caravans. He loathed them. But he knew this was an individual issue and ought not to influence him in his elected role. He said that he had tried to overcome his prejudice, but he was aware that it was constantly clouding his judgment on planning issues, and this made his contribution to the committee inappropriate. So he had decided that it was best to resign. Oh, that we were all so honest and brave and candid!

Shami Chakrabarti says the secret of independence is to make it clear that you are always prepared to walk away in the end. Brandon Gough says you have to be close enough to read the tea leaves, so that you anticipate the snares and traps that could cause you to lose your independence. Michael Bichard has an even cruder definition: "*Independent is if you haven't been captured*" (again, useful idiots come to mind). Julie Baddeley says she grapples with the notion of independence in her board positions: "*You are there to be an independent. The trouble is that, to deliver on this, you have to maintain a certain distance and therefore have a limited window onto the organization. On the other hand, you know that, to be any real use on strategy, you need to know quite a lot about the business. It is a tricky balancing act, and how well it works depends very much on how the Chair runs the board. One major thing you do bring is knowledge from the outer circles. This is very valuable, because it is amazing how little external perspective is discussed in the boardroom."* David Varney agrees that it is tough: *"In the core circle, on the whole, your strength, your power, comes from your knowledge and your experience. In the outer circles, it is your vulnerability that is your strength. The vulnerability of not knowing enough but of being able to provide a fresh eye, so that you formulate the right questions and forge the right linkages so that you open things up."*

And John Inge goes further: *"You must not just be independent of all the forces out there, but those inside you too. Too many leaders are dismally lacking in self-awareness. They are often driven by their own personal agenda. Independence is not just about being independent of thought and of others, but also of yourself."* John remembers once sitting next to a Nobel prize winner and discovering that, far from any great thoughts about humanity, the man had really wanted to prove his father wrong. Seamus McAleavey talks about the day when he thinks Tony Blair lost so much support in Northern Ireland. He came out of a crucial meeting to face the cameras with: *"This is not a time for soundbites. I feel the hand of history on my shoulder."* Seamus is clear that he opened himself to ridicule and distrust because people spotted that there was something else going on there.

Your personal brand

You need to put a lot of effort into branding. This means establishing, quite separately from the brand you represent in your core role, your own personal brand. As Michael Bichard says: *"A problem for many leaders is that they define their brand according to the role they play in their box: their organization, their job. They also need a brand for themselves, decided by them, free of the box. Just as people buy from a brand they trust, people listen to one they trust. You have to put great effort into deciding what it is, then building it and guarding it. Because people will want it and they will want to link it to what they are passionate about."*

David Puttnam is interesting about personal brands: *"The lovely thing about the outer circles is that all that really matters there is influence. And influence travels. You can't transfer authority from one circle to another – but you can transfer influence. And influence is mainly about character. I believe that your influence increases if you behave properly and if you do what you say you will do."*

You also need to make your personal brand really about you and not just a load of words stolen from some book. The word transparency comes to mind. People always tell me that you need to be completely open and endlessly "transparent." It has become an almost unquestioned item on the branding list for the outer circle. But, in truth, I would not follow someone who had transparency on their list. Sure, I want honesty, but not always transparency. Think about a game of poker (not a bad analogy for the outer circles). Pulling a card from your sleeve is cheating – it's dishonest. But bluffing, which has very little to do with transparency, is part of the game. If you can't bluff, you'll never get anywhere.

Protecting your brand

You have to take great care of your brand because you don't want it to be ruined – least of all for a petty reason. It is agony watching it being damaged, especially when you can't do anything about it. Michael Bichard thinks that if you fail to protect it when you are leading beyond your authority, then you pretty well have to get back into your core circle. He has good advice on both choosing and protecting your brand:

❑ Beware of advisers. Remember, you are the one who will get rubbished and ridiculed, and it won't be any good if you say you did it because your advisers told you to. You have to decide branding issues for yourself.
❑ Watch out for flattery and flak. But also look out for your own personal ambition, because sometimes it can lead you to do the wrong things.
❑ If you go out on a public platform, it must always be to say something new and stimulating. Don't tell the audience what they knew before you arrived.
❑ Watch out for when you are just going through the motions. This is when you are at your most dangerous – and it's when you need to watch yourself carefully.

Others add to Michael's list. Carolyn Berkeley is Chair of Enfield Primary Care Trust. She makes a point that is close to Michael's: *"Usually, we undermine our brand not by doing deliberately bad things, but shabby things."*

Tim Jones is a Director of Capital One Bank (Europe) plc. He adds:

"In deciding your brand, you need to keep in mind that you have to be you. Don't create a fake you, because it will become very obvious very fast." Pretty well everyone makes the same point in different ways. David Puttnam: *"What you say needs to be the same thing as what you do."* And Jude Kelly: *"How you do things needs to be the same as what you are trying to do."*

Sarah Ebanja is Group Director at the London Development Agency. She is pretty sick of what she sees as wishy-washy words. I was speaking alongside her a while ago. When someone mentioned the word values, she replied: *"I don't care about your values. I am sick to death of hearing about people's values. What I want is for you to tell me about your standards. What will you accept? And what won't you? When will you make a stand? On what issue? And when?"*

A chief constable who does not want to be named (and I can understand why) says: *"Choose your fights with government carefully. Politicians deal with threats by rubbishing you and they are very good at it."* If you make a mistake in the political arena, it is likely that your personal brand will be in tatters.

Sir Gerry Robinson is Chair of Moto Hospitality Ltd. When he became a Common Purpose trustee, he gave me a piece of advice on what he expected of me as a chief executive. I have never forgotten it: *"I don't pay you to say yes to people. I pay you to say no and at the right times. It is one of the problems of success. Everyone can think of all the other amazing things you should be doing. Somehow you have to do the right ones, and be brave enough, and independent enough, to say no to the wrong ones. Only then do you protect your brand."*

Shami Chakrabarti says it's the compromises you make that will most decide your brand: *"This is what we will be judged on. The real art is to know what to make concessions on, when to make them – and when not to. What's a good compromise and what's a bad one."* She suspects that history probably judges you by your bad ones and says that you decide them by: *"having it very clear in your mind what your brand stands for. You have to keep going back to your values and your objectives and not be distracted from them."* Dr. Musharraf Hussain agrees: *"How do you judge a good compromise? If it doesn't violate your basic principles and the other party has had to move too. Of course, compromises are very difficult for minorities. As a minority, an outsider, you feel weak and you sometimes justify things on the basis of the lesser of two evils. You become defensive and are sometimes willing to make very big compromises, and settle for less."*

Independence is everything at the outset

If you are setting up something new in the outer circles, then you need to treat its branding in the same way as your own, because its brand will become associated with yours.

The messages come through:

- ❑ Who you choose to involve: the trustees, the supporters (the backers inside or out), and the people you involve or employ.
- ❑ Where you choose to be based. What message will this send out? Who will you be assumed to be aligning with by being there?
- ❑ How you are funded. Where did the money come from? Does one source dominate? Is anyone paying the piper and calling the tunes?

For Common Purpose, at the start, independence was crucial. The trustees produced a message of independence and I remember, long before I met Anita Roddick and Brandon Gough, going to see Betty Boothroyd, who was then Speaker of the House of Commons. In those days, you showed how independent you were as an organization by having just about everyone on your board, especially the right numbers from all the political parties. She advised me to have all or none, but better none. Otherwise you spend your whole time calibrating your independence, rather than just stating it.

The office was borrowed from Anita Roddick. The funding came in small amounts from ten sources so that no single one dominated. I well remember having to hand back a check for £250,000 from one of the first sponsors, who believed passionately in the idea. It would have put an end to our independence, real or perceived, so I asked the sponsor to rewrite it for £30,000.

Rudi Bogni is a director of Old Mutual plc and Prospect Publishing. He believes that we need many, many more small organizations that are very independent: *"In Italy, there is almost no trust in leaders. The expectations are low and that's what we get. Of course, with these levels of trust, the system becomes almost unworkable. I have backed a small think tank that is serious, has integrity, and communicates well. You need 100 more of these to produce change. They all need to avoid taking government money, aligning themselves consciously or unconsciously, and they must not start to convince themselves that they can influence things by playing party politics rather than through rigorous thought."*

Not in it for yourself

In the outer circles, you can't be in it for yourself. Prue Leith puts it simply: *"You have to give everyone the credit, except yourself."* Sue Stapely is equally blunt: *"It cannot be about building your own profile or bank balance."* It was put beautifully to me by the author and social philosopher Charles Handy when he returned from an OpenGround gathering, where he had observed me way out of my comfort zone: *"You need to keep on living vicariously for the triumphs of others, taking secret pleasure in their achievements that only you know you have played a part in."*

Sandy Forrest, ever the policeman, talks about keeping your fingerprints off your successes. He has stuck to this principle through thick and thin with the partnerships he has worked on: *"Delegate the credit. If you do, your partners will trust you, because you do not threaten their self-esteem or their organizational credibility. If they trust you, a virtuous circle develops and they are keen to work with you again. You need to learn to internalize success, to know the value of your role even if it is not apparent to others. It requires a goodly measure of pre-existing self-confidence."*

Jude Kelly says it's about *"giving away gifts."* Janet Paraskeva adds: *"and your partner has to be of the same view too. They must not be demanding the credit and recognition when you get home at night."* Gill Morgan says it is really, in the end, about *"the principle of goodness. If you do something good for someone, it gets passed on, and someone does something good for someone else and, in the end, it always comes back, even if it is not from the person you were originally good to. It's far too simple, but it helps."*

The last word on independence should perhaps go to a journalist. Simon Fanshawe, who was active in starting Stonewall, says: *"It will fail if it is selfish. To gain legitimacy, it has to be beyond our own narrow self-interest. Stonewall was not just about giving gays a leg up. It was about human rights for us all, the kind of fairness that everyone is entitled to in a decent society. If you don't get this right, you lay yourself open. People will try to find the ax you are grinding, your selfishness, or how you will benefit. They will assume that you are protecting your own interests, or that you are in it for either money or credit."*

THE RIGHT APPROACH 4: PASSION AND RESONANCE

Beyond your authority, you have to have passion. It comes in different forms. Mine is direct, loud, and demanding. Yours may be softly spoken, private, and understated. But passion is what people long for in their leaders. So, in the outer circles, stick to issues you can feel passion for in your own way. As David Simon says: *"You watch out for the passionate because they will produce great change. They will never give up. They care deeply."* Paddy Ashdown agrees: *"The main reason I took on the task in Bosnia was that I love the place with a passion."* This was no doubt self-evident to all those who came across him, in good times and bad. Back to David Simon, who says that people will forgive everything, including the excesses, of the passionate, because: *"Passion comes from the heart. Sometimes passion goes wrong, because you have gone over the top, but people will forgive you, because it comes from the heart. You may sometimes lose a battle, but people won't actually go out and try to subvert the passionate. At most, you will create anti-momentum, but no more. It's hard to subvert passion; it's much easier to fight cool methodology."* Stranger One agrees: *"You can rubbish passion – and if you do, you make them even more passionate – but you can't undermine it."*

A scientist who went on the Common Purpose program in Nottingham once told me about his newly formed view on power and passion. As a physicist, he had distinct ideas about power: *"Generally, leaders in the city seem to see power as something you slice up, dividing it in different ways according to beliefs and experience. I see power and energy as things you create. It's not about dividing up a cake. It's about expanding it and creating ever more power, with passion as its source."*

Passion can get in the way

The trouble is that you can get it so wrong. You can inadvertently switch up the volume too high. You may get it wrong because you are passionately excited by something, when really you need to be cool and dispassionate if you are going to persuade others. Sometimes, it's because you get passionately angry about something that seems so meaningless (or inappropriate, or pompous, or even duplicitous), and really you need to be cutting and clipped if you are going to get people out of your way. Passion can certainly be unhelpful. I went to see

David Puttnam a while ago, so that he could give me feedback on a meeting where I had messed up. I got very angry (and I was right to be angry) but I was not at all clever about dealing with it. His advice was: *"Never go into a meeting unless you know the one thing you want out of it. And, for the rest of the meeting, be absolutely delightful."* Of course, because he too is passionate, he did admit that he frequently forgets to take his own advice.

Resonance

In the outer circles, you have to become "multilingual" (as Moira Wallace calls it) and learn to speak enough different languages that you can get your passion across in all of them. There is the language of the general public, of opinion formers, and of the media. It is interesting that many of the greats at leading beyond authority speak more than one national language: they don't just shout louder when they need to be heard – and understood – by different audiences. You have to find ways to resonate, to express yourself so that people start nodding before you have finished speaking. As Gill Morgan says: *"Whoever you are with, you have to be constantly asking yourself, why would they ...? Why would they agree with this? Why would they go there? Why would they say that? Why would they back off? All the time, it's about 'why would they?' and never about 'what or why would I?'* And, if you end up at loggerheads with someone, you have to get outside yourself and look at the two of you from a third observer's position and ask: "What would I say was the problem here?"* Gill has to resonate: this is where her legitimacy comes from. She has to listen very, very hard and then resonate so that the enormously disparate community that forms the membership of the NHS Confederation will go with her.

Before I first met Sandy Forrest, I had heard from many other police officers that he was very effective in a siege situation. I asked him why. How did he manage to tempt people out when others might find it hard? Where did he find the words and ideas that resonated? He said that when he was a child his mother was always telling him to stop speaking to everyone and to hurry up. As a young constable on the beat, he always used every opportunity provided by his uniform to speak to as many people as possible. He had accumulated masses and masses of conversations over his life, and in siege situations they all came back to him, so that he understood people, and could think through what would resonate in different situations.

Jane Campbell feels the same. She really takes the time to know people: *"I have had the huge advantage, because of my disability and physical dependency, of having been intimate with over 100 people during my life. It means you are thrown into a situation where you get to know people on a very personal basis and knowing people like this makes you very much more effective in the outer circles."*

Shami Chakrabarti says the same about resonating: *"I spend my time trying to minimize the differences between myself and my audience, so that I minimize the difference between us and our interests. Then, hopefully, I come across as more reasonable and so more convincing."*

When you see Shami on the television and your eyes wander over the audience, you will see people who only an hour ago might have written off her views as political correctness begin to nod. They are not simply in agreement with her. Some, you can see, are really proud of her. Her resonance comes from the power of her ideas and from her passion, personal qualities, and powers of persuasion. She has found a way to make them resonate. She finds out about her audience. If she talks about identity cards, with one audience she will concentrate on discrimination and, with another, it will be about freedom: *"People expect activists to use words like 'disgusting' and 'outrageous.' So I use words like 'inappropriate' and 'unconstitutional.'"*

As she says: *"You have to find a way into people's own language and values in order to appeal to them."* I asked her what is crucial if you are going to resonate in the UK. She says that you have to self-deprecate; it's a subset of politeness for the British: *"You have to show regard for others, rather than for yourself. It's also good lightly to tease yourself, undermine yourself just a little, and not take yourself too seriously."* She also says that *"you might as well get used to it, your resonating in the UK comes from your expertise, your universality, your heritage, your Britishness, and your ability so use them and combine them to best effect."*

Tim Jones says that it's exactly the same if you are leading beyond your authority but within your own organization. He has what he calls a doctrine of minimal novelty: *"You're in enough trouble as it is, doing something new! Make sure you only introduce the essential minimum of novelty in your proposal: avoid unnecessary novelty like the plague. This will help others see you as balanced, rather than as someone who likes to do things differently for the sake of being different. Present your idea as the same, even if it isn't."* When he was at NatWest, he and a few others came up with the idea of a new payment scheme that became known as Switch. He explains that *"you have to fit in to be able to change things, and this includes looking the part."* Bankers in the City of London do not wear bow ties; they wear proper ties, tied in the proper fashion. *"You simply cannot afford to be the only person in the bank wearing a bow tie. If you want to produce change, you have to resonate – and with your appearance too. If you do become the banker with the bow tie, you won't be able to change anything."*

Tim Jones agrees with Shami: *"To bring about change you have to have cultural resonance. You have to not just be trying to change things from within as a transformer, but you have to fit in as much as you can."* As Michael Bichard says: *"If you have something to say, you need to work hard to say it in a way that people will listen."* Then again, as Peter Tatchell says, don't go out to reach everyone: *"You have to be realistic. You have to accept, especially in the outer circles where there are so many different audiences, that what resonates for one person won't necessarily resonate for another."*

Communicating the passion

If you are going to lead beyond authority, you cannot delegate the communication. A while ago, I spoke alongside a young man who is considered to be (indeed, is being groomed as) a future leader of a very big international company. I was deeply shocked by how badly he spoke in public. He lacked passion and made little attempt to resonate. It was not about the audience or the individual occasion – it was a basic lack of skills. When I pushed him, he said that, on the whole, he could employ people to cover this weakness that he knew he had. Basically, he had accepted that it was not one of his strengths and he avoided public speaking whenever he could. I believe that, until he masters this, he will only ever excel in his core circle. There are plenty of training courses he could go on, but what he really needs to do is recognize the need and speak so often in public that he eventually masters the art.

When I first went to the Industrial Society, I watched John Garnett. He was probably the best orator of his day. People were transfixed; so much of his legitimacy came entirely from his speeches. Whole generations heard him and still comment to this day on his impact. I watched him and learnt as much as I could. About pace and silences. About whispering. About always laughing with your audience, even if it's you they are laughing at. Then I bought the tapes of Martin Luther King's speeches and Winston Churchill's; I listened to them in the car and learnt about the power of repetition and about building up your argument. Of course you have to avoid the "We will fight them on the beaches" tone, but the tapes give you much more than this. All those speeches were so well thought through and structured – they were never off the cuff. Sure, it's fun to hear after-dinner speakers who ramble on and make you laugh, but you seldom remember the message the next morning. John said I had to master the art, so he sent me all around the country. It was Industry Year – a year in which to celebrate the contribution of industry to society – and I was told to do 40 speeches to Women's Institutes about the importance of industry. After the first 20, I got really quite good. This skill is worth mastering. It is oddly rare – but it gives you huge legitimacy. Sometimes even exaggerated legitimacy and authority.

Richard Bowker agrees about the importance of communication: *"You have to learn that your way is not the only way. I learnt this through bitter experience at the Strategic Rail Authority. Once I had got it, then I became far more effective. Emotional intelligence becomes far more important: the ability to communicate, sell, and get buy-in. Take the example of the West Coast line. We decided, perfectly rationally, that we could not do the work in the evening – it would take years. We had to be brave and shut down whole sections at a time. This involved closing Stoke-on-Trent station completely for four months. However rational the case, we had to make it good news for Stoke somehow. We spent a very long time figuring out how to do this. It seemed a bit of a tall order. How could losing your main rail station for four months be good news? But we did and, on the announcement day, when I went on Stoke local radio station (rather than on the main national morning news in London), we were greeted with 'There is good news for Stoke this morning!' It's not rocket science, but you can get so obsessed with the logic of the plan and argument that you don't see the simple stuff."*

The media is an audience too

And you need to learn to communicate with the media. As Derek Higgs says: *"You need to learn how to react to the media when you are a hot news story. If you don't know, you will keel over. The pressure under the spotlight is like a maelstrom. Sadly, it is often a self-taught learning curve; you have to learn to cope when you are in totally uncontrollable situations."* Michael Bichard agrees – but says you can prepare for it. He learnt a lot from chairing the Soham inquiry: *"I made a huge effort to work with the media right from the start, because I realized that they would be the mouthpiece for the eventual report. I gave the journalists a high quality service all the way through and dealt with them as intelligent human beings. The report itself was then very lean with about 30 points, of which five were the crucial ones."*

Grow a thick skin

While you are polishing your communication skills, start to develop a thick skin. Michael Bichard describes his shock when he encountered open hatred from someone who disagreed with his inquiry's conclusions. And Derek Higgs warns: *"You will not be the first or last person to suffer from the propensity of many to venture opinions on your work untroubled by the need for information, let alone the courtesy of getting their facts right. And the press is only a mirror. If the wind of opinion is blowing hard in a single direction, that is what will appear tomorrow morning, whatever you say – and irrespective of the facts or judgment of the writer. Colorful quotes will be taken out of context to support a story of 'controversy' or 'anger' at the expense of some debate about serious issues. The only practical response is to develop a few more layers of skin on a broad back."*

SCENARIO: OWNING PROBLEMS, ORDERING PRIORITIES

You are Chair of Governors at a primary school. Early this morning, you heard that one of your students was killed last night in what looks like a racially motivated attack. You are a director of a multinational company; male, black, 35, single – and stunned. Everyone wants everything from you now: the police, the local community, local government, local, national, and international media, parents at the school, the family of the boy, leaders in the black community, the head, the staff, your colleagues at work, your friends, local and national politicians, the Department of Education. How do you decide who owns which problems and what to prioritize?

Lord Hastings is International Director of Corporate Citizenship at KPMG.

I think the Chair of Governors has a moral duty, on behalf of the school, to contact and seek to support the parents as quickly as possible. But it is essential that this does not get the Chair as an individual, or the school generally, embroiled in public responsibility for the crime or the perpetrators. This problem does not belong to the school and it should not seek to absorb the pressure. If it does, it takes to itself the consequences of actions undertaken offsite within a community where the rough edges are not the creation or purpose of the school. The school too is a victim of this context; it must not become its spokesperson or seek – alone – to provide the solutions.

Susan Liautaud is Associate Dean of Stanford Law School.

I believe the top priorities for the Chair of Governors would be:

1. Ensure full cooperation with law enforcement authorities.
2. Address needs for additional school security.
3. Seek expert advice on – and implement assistance for – the emotional needs of the school community.
4. Communicate succinctly and factually the school's actions: privately to the family, within the school community, and through the media to the larger community (without conjecture or commentary on non-school parties or actions).

All of this requires gathering the governors and school staff. Then, the Chair of Governors should consider how, going forward, the school community and board of Governors might best contribute to problem solving: supporting the family and school community in healing.

I do not believe the analysis should focus on "who owns which problems." The key questions are: who can positively contribute to solving the problems, and how are tasks most effectively allocated? As Chair of Governors, I should seek to lead the school community in its appropriate participation in a problem-solving effort through the circles mentioned, rather than shrink from "ownership." While the fact that the incident happened off of school grounds might absolve the school of some legal responsibility, the location of the incident is irrelevant to the impact of a murdered child on the family and school community, and, therefore, to the school's reaction beyond legal action.

Peter Sherratt is Managing Director, Lehman Brothers, and Chair of Governors, Oaklands School.

I would go to the school and help the headteacher to liaise with the police to make sure they have everything they need to do their job. If the student who was killed has a sibling at the school, we must make sure that he or she is safe. If the police want to question other students, we must help them to do this, but ask that, as far as possible, it is done in a way which is calm and thoughtful about the impact that will have on the rest of the school.

If the victim's family would like to talk over the phone, I would do that straight away, but could only agree to meet them after attending to the police and the immediate needs of the school and government.

I would check with local and national government to see if they need anything specific to be done immediately and, if so, do it. Otherwise, I would wait to engage them in a more detailed dialog later in the day, after dealing with the school.

I would ask the police to handle the media. The student wasn't killed while at school, and the school's – and therefore my – priority is not to deal with the media, but to think about its students and their parents.

Then I would talk to the head about what to say to the staff and the pupils. This is a time for the leadership of the school to be calm and careful about how to react. We should not rush to a conclusion about what motivated the attack, and we should make sure that people focus their attention on the victim and the victim's family, and put aside all thoughts of how to react against the criminals.

Bola Ogun is Operations Manager at Imperial Tobacco Ltd and Chair of Governors, Oliver Goldsmith School.

This actually happened to me a few years ago. I was phoned by the headteacher. I was in New York on a business trip, and he woke me at 5am.

Only as I got to the airport, and my friends began to phone me, and I saw the headlines in the newspapers, did I really understand just how difficult this was going to be. By the time I got to the school, everyone was traipsing all over it and the media were camped outside. You can't begin to understand what it is like to be besieged by the media until you experience having 30 or more reporters and journalists from TV, radio, and the local and national press with their mikes, cameras with telescopic lenses, bright lights, flash guns, dictating machines, pads, and satellite link-ups thrusting from every direction straight at you. They blocked every phone line with calls and approached everyone who came near the school in a relentless quest for a new angle on the story. In the midst of this, a whole range of national politicians, public dignitaries (including ambassadors), and people from public bodies came to visit.

My first response was disbelief and sadness at the tragic loss of life. Then anger at the allegations that were being thrown around. Of course, I had my own personal views about what might have happened – but I knew I had to suspend them until I had some evidence.

I knew that it was up to the Governors to own the problem from the school's point of view, so I immediately called a Governors' meeting.

Deciding the priorities was much harder. Looking back, I think I made two mistakes:

❑   Controlling the communication, as far as was possible, was key. Saying nothing was not an option. But it took me a little while to realize that some organizations that appeared to be offering help were actually doing so knowing that their agendas were in conflict with ours and wanting to get their own message across. I quickly decided that we would do our own communication instead. I think maybe Peter and Susan might have fallen naively into the same trap as I originally did.

❑ I realized – too late – that all the players involved had their own agenda, and that taking their advice at face value was not sensible. This is a hard one because, in such a situation, you do want some "friends" but, somehow, you have to resist the temptation to look for them. For example, I took the police advice about not going to visit the parents. I should not have done – I should have followed my own instincts and visited them. Part of the reason why I didn't was about me; I don't have children myself so I felt, in some ways, that I couldn't understand the enormity of their loss and therefore was not the right person for them at the time. Of course, with hindsight, this was entirely wrong.

Looking back I would say that the priorities should be:

1. Express sympathy to the family and ignore all advice to the contrary.
2. Find answers to all the questions you can find answers for. So that you have them for all the people who will, quite rightly, be asking them.
3. Convene the governing body and get on with owning the problem (I don't agree with Michael Hastings on this). Schools are a key focal point in neighborhoods and should help the community through challenging times.

I would also say that very little had ever happened to me in my core circle that prepared me for this situation.

IT'S ABOUT PEOPLE 1: INTEREST

Human interest

All the best exponents of leading beyond their authority have a profound interest in people. I don't mean individuals, but people generally: human beings. Such an interest cannot be pretended – it either rings true or it doesn't. It gives these leaders integrity and authenticity. When you meet them, they come out to meet you (physically perhaps, but also in their approach). When you leave them, you do so knowing they have listened to you and they have carefully checked their understanding (making sure they know what you have said, not just what they might want to have heard). You feel scrutinized. They never glaze over, not once, and they never make assumptions about you. While you are with them, you know you are the most important person in the world for them. You leave feeling bigger, you walk tall. As people said of John Garnett: "*He bothered enough about people.*"

Too often you meet people who do not see you as a person in your own right: they only see you in relation to themselves, as an extra in their scene rather than as a fellow character who is worth taking time to understand. The best leaders beyond authority take the opposite approach. Susan Hitch is manager of Lord Sainsbury's trust. As she puts it: "*They look you in the eye and know it's you. They see other people as whole people, with many facets, some that they may like or rate and some that they won't, and not just the ten-minute glimpsed version when they met. They see others' ideas, what they think, how they think. And it's not about liking people – it's about building a bond with them that will mean that all future engagements, however small, will add more value to both parties.*"

And you need to feel this whoever you are, young or old. As Narayana Murthy says: "*I revere youth. After all, that's where the energy and enthusiasm are and where the new ideas come from, the ideas that will challenge the status quo.*"

Relationships in a nanosecond

The best leaders in the outer circles can create relationships in a nanosecond. They meet new people and, before you know it, they have created an instant relationship that most people would take hours (if not days) to build. Many tell me that this is one of the stunning things that Tony Blair and Bill Clinton have in common.

Younger leaders can do this virtually, over the web, in the same way. Instantly.

Managing the relationships

The best don't just establish relationships – they take the trouble to maintain them. I am told that Bill Clinton would always know your name and your interests whenever he crossed your path again. As Gill Morgan says: *"You have to actively manage your relationships. Take time over people. Even if, at this point, there is nothing you are trying to achieve together."* Jude Kelly agrees: *"You have to have faith in the meetings with no apparent outcome. If you build the relationships and the trust, then all the details will come together and stick together fast, if and when you need them to."*

With everyone?

Do you have to do this with everyone? Even the people you don't respect or don't like? Paddy Ashdown says this is where business leaders always come unstuck beyond their authority: *"Why have so few brilliant businessmen made brilliant politicians? Because they haven't learnt to suffer fools gladly."*

In your core circle, people you consider to be fools can be moved aside or out. In the outer circles, you do not have the authority to remove anyone. So you have to learn to cope with them, at least to get them onside. They can cause you damage. They can harm your cause. They can delay you and stop you in your tracks.

Sometimes, as you engage with them, you discover that they are not really fools at all. In the outer circles – where everything is so unfamiliar, where power comes in different forms, and leaders have such varying agendas – you can't always spot them at first blink. Indeed, sometimes they are just playing fools because it suits them.

I think it helps in dealing with fools if you have been treated as a fool yourself. If you know what it is like to be patronized, or dismissed. To be made to feel a fool and to discover how rapidly you become one, if that's what people expect of you.

Why does this matter?

Because it's through new relationships that you get new learning. As you go into the outer circles, you have to learn fast. Because, in the absence of authority, you have to be able to seduce people. To do this you have to know them and care about them. Because, in new spaces, you need to be able to spot talent and engage it. If you are not interested in people, it will pass you by.

A young colleague used to work as a researcher at the World Economic Forum (otherwise known as Davos). Before that, she was at Procter & Gamble, chosen for her brains and charm, which must have stood out a mile amongst the candidates. She talks about meeting the leaders as they arrived at the annual Davos Forum and being treated like a flunkey. They would glance at her and ask her about lavatories and coats and power points. They would never look her in the eye and take in that she was not an assistant. She is short, young, female, and brown skinned – they no doubt had her well categorized in their minds. They could never quite be bothered to look harder. My experience of her indicates that they would have found her fascinating.

As Stranger Two says: *"You have to believe that people have something to offer, even if it seems unlikely, even if it's just so that you can see their angle. You have to believe, because you can't pretend to."*

The "no people"

My problem always used to be with the "no people." But, over the years, I have learnt to listen to them hard. Because then you get an insight into what you are up against. They are the people who can always give you 15,000 reasons why what you are proposing to do will not work, or is not worth trying. If you are lucky, you find great "no people." In the early years of Common Purpose, I used to go quite regularly to see Lord Dahrendorf to pick his brains. He had been the Director of the London School of Economics when I was there. He was a clever man who knew how the world worked. I would tell him what I wanted to do next – and he would tell me all the reasons why it would not work. Then, next time we met, I would tell him that it had worked. He would be utterly delighted and we would proceed to discuss the next undertaking. He was an invaluable source of understanding of risk and obstacles so that I could prepare to go over, under, round, or right through them.

You need "no people" – but not too many, and not too often. If you are not careful, they will frighten you and persuade you to give up. Because they can be deeply undermining and hard to deal with. Best to find "no people" like Lord Dahrendorf: those who want you to succeed and actually take pleasure in being proved wrong.

Opposers are easier. At least people who are opposing you have some momentum. Your task is to turn their momentum to join with yours (or join them if you discover you were wrong). There is energy about them. With "no people," there is a total lack of energy. Opposers will produce something you don't necessarily want; "no people" will stop anything from happening by squandering everyone's energy.

Transmit and receive

If you haven't got this profound interest in people, can you acquire it? Maybe not. But I think you can spark it or re-ignite it if it's there. Tom Frawley says: *"Be available. Go to unlikely places and listen hard."* My father would say *"Switch the wireless from transmit to receive."* Sandy Forrest would no doubt suggest that you join the police and go out on the beat: *"Then you will see how people react, especially in situations of high tension. Everyone has buttons which, if pressed, will prompt different reactions. The better you know people, the better you know the buttons and how to press them. This knowledge and experience comes in handy when you are trying to achieve something through people who do not need to do what you say."*

IT'S ABOUT PEOPLE 2: NETWORKS

Networks: good or bad?

We all have networks. It is sad that, nowadays, the word conjures up images of self-serving, nasty people who are entirely out for themselves – who are building connections with people and seeking success by scratching each other's backs. In organizations, people think of "networkers" as over-ambitious, slightly lightweight creeps. In society, we think that networks are what keep others out. We associate them with elites and exclusion: there to ensure that only those who are "in" stay in power. They keep nepotism alive and well. Journalists sneer at networks because they embody closeness and lack of transparency and many of the incestuous things about power that they became journalists to try to challenge. Much of the time, they are right. But the danger is that, in denigrating networks, we lose a piece of connectivity in society that we badly need. And it's this connectivity that is so crucial in producing the sense of belonging which enables people to add value, either to the organization they work in or to the society they live in.

I would like to suggest two criteria for testing whether networks are positive before opposing or ridiculing them. One: the network needs to be about something bigger than the individuals involved. And two: the purpose of the network must not be to exclude others.

Nothing happens without networks

I cannot see how anything happens without networks. How do people ever gather around a great idea and make it happen? Recently, I was reading Bill Bryson's *A Short History of Nearly Everything*. How wonderful to discover that one set of scientists were working for over two years to get rid of some background noise on their instruments. They simply could not figure out where it came from or how to get rid of it. Meanwhile, another set of scientists, down the road, were determined that the noise from the Big Bang must still be out there, reverberating in the universe. It took two of the scientists who were working on the projects to meet in a bar to find out that they had both discovered the solution to each other's problem. The noise on the first project's instruments was the echoing of the Big Bang. I am not arguing for more bars, but I am arguing for more time hearing about each other's issues and seeing if two and two could just make more than four this time (rather than the usual three).

Necessary networks

Organizations need networks so that people can see each other's issues and ideas, spot new ones, and see the risks that are not simply confined to one area. We need the areas around the water coolers, the lunch areas, the staff events that get everyone together. Then they all discover that not everyone in manufacturing is brainless, and not everyone in sales is a creep, and they start to grab opportunities that emerge because sales and manufacturing got together.

We also need civic networks: so that citizens can gather and exchange and find ways to combine their efforts. The Ancient Greeks had market squares in the center of their cities where they met to discuss and form and reform ideas. They called them *agoras*. OK, they kept the slaves and the women out – which meant that they failed to gather all the talent available and missed many opportunities as a result. But they met – and took the time to do it. We need many more opportunities to do this today. Not simply at the community level, but at all levels. So that we can ask the difficult questions of our leaders, keep the big issues on the agenda, and work together when we see that something needs doing. Whether it is holding our local politicians to account on a planning issue, or demanding that our national politicians don't duck difficult issues like pensions, or trying to get environmental issues on the world political agenda. John Inge asks: *"When did civic friendship become nepotism?"* How have we allowed citizens networking, learning about each other, developing ideas together, standing up and being counted together, to turn into something which is threatening and elitist, rather than an example of democracy at work?

Two types of network

If we are to dust down the word "networks" and allow ourselves to develop them, we need to take the time to develop two types: "support" networks and "turbulence" networks. The former need to be full of people who will encourage us, egg us on, be there for us, watch our backs, and believe in us – especially when we move outside our comfort zone, our core circle. And the latter are with people who will tell us the truth and tell us what we don't want to hear (or can't hear any more). People who will tell us when we are getting too big for our boots and who warn us when we are beginning to believe our own rubbish. Both support and turbulence networks need working on and nourishing. Tom Frawley says he seeks a combination of the two:

"The best networks are full of people from outside your world, but who know it. They can see the bigger picture and they understand it. They also have no ax to grind and are not prisoners of one interest group. Then of course they must be prepared to tell you the truth."

The lost art

One of the problems is that networking seems to take so much time. Maybe that's because people have got out of the habit of simply meeting new people and getting to know them. Often you go to events and find very grand people waiting to be spoken to. Some are too grand and are simply a lost cause. But many are simply out of the habit, or just shy. They would not for a minute consider going up and introducing themselves to someone they didn't already know.

If you watch the best leaders beyond their authority work a room, you realize that, like working the courage muscle, this just needs practice. They will move around and learn fast. When you speak to them, you know they are really interested in you because of the way they look at you and hear you, and how they stand and smile and encourage you. As a result, of course, you will tell them anything they want – and even more if they choose to confide in you. The greats, says Roisín McDonough: *"come into a gathering and, within ten minutes, they have tuned into the mood in the room."*

These skills need finding – or rediscovering. As someone admitted to me when he was starting to lead beyond his authority: *"I realized that I had done absolutely no networking. I did go to events, but I rarely actually spoke to anyone and even if I did I never followed up."* Michael Bichard would tell him to get over this reticence – and get stuck in: *"You need your networks so that people will listen to you, give you feedback, contribute to your thinking, and most importantly, allow you to influence them. I have been direct, some would say abrasive all my life. It seems strange that people now see me as such a great networker!"*

Some leaders simply slide into bad habits. They have long forgotten the secrets of grabbing a plate of food and offering it around until they find someone interesting to talk to and then stopping there. Have they forgotten about smiling? That, if they look fearsome or miserable, no one will want to talk to them? They may have moved beyond the days of fumbling for their card, but have they forgotten the old trick of wearing an unusual tie or scarf so that people can approach them and talk about the tie or scarf to get the conversation going?

Have they taken the trouble to introduce people to each other properly – which allows them to move on to someone else? Have they fallen into the bad habit of glancing over someone's shoulder to see if there is anyone else to talk to? Have they got out of the good habit of making their small talk more interesting than the weather and what other people do for a living?

They need to regain it all – and set themselves targets before they go into a room. How many new people are they are going to meet? How many old relationships are they going to nurture? And how many new ideas are they going to grapple with? So that they don't get tempted to revert to grandness – or retreat into shyness.

Force yourself

Maybe it's not grandness or shyness. Maybe these leaders simply never learnt the skills. And I blame the parents! Three of my children will go up to anyone. Two of them won't and we have had to make it pretty clear to them that they have to. Not as much as their siblings, who find it easy, but a lot more than they would naturally. When they were small, if they did not greet strangers we introduced them to by putting their hands out to shake and looking the stranger in the eye, they were off to bed. The temptation to look at the floor was compelling – but they didn't much want to look at the bedroom walls either.

My father went even further. I remember him having a go at me for not speaking to someone I was sitting next to at dinner. I was ten – and he was furious. He asked me why I had been so rude and I said what many ten-year-olds might have said: *"He was boring."* Then my father explained that I had just spent two hours sitting next to a man who, had I taken the trouble to find out, was a world expert on a certain type of tropical fish. In fact, I had probably just missed the only opportunity I would ever have in my entire life to grill an expert about this type of tropical fish. Would this information ever come in handy? Maybe, one day. But I had missed the opportunity, come what may.

Have I failed my father's test since? Often. With my husband, who is fascinated about science and how things work. But most of the time, I don't fail him. And, as a result, I think I can network faster than most.

Avoiding "group think"

You need to make sure that the new networks you develop are not just more of the same. Providing more support – and not enough turbulence. Beware of discovering more people who think like you –

and not enough who see the world from another angle. Who read different books, websites, and newspapers. Whose instincts vary from yours. The danger is that people gravitate towards people that they feel comfortable with. That will just reinforce the "group think."

The most closed network I was ever invited to join started when a friend (also called Julia) celebrated her fiftieth birthday by inviting all her friends called Julia to dinner. There were 14 of us. It was great fun (because she has great friends) but it was also confusing: *"Oh what an interesting point Julia, and I know Julia agrees, but what does Julia think about it ...."* The danger is that our networks, far from serving us, begin to limit us.

Reset your bandwidth

Think of radar. You tend to choose a narrow setting for the beam, because there is a limit to the amount of information you want to take in. You know bleeps would also come from outside that narrow beam, but you have decided not to take them in. I think it's worth thinking about your networks in this sense. How narrow can you afford to set your screen? Can you limit the information you are receiving too much? Are you hearing what people who are not familiar to you are saying? People who tend not to agree with you, or see the world differently from you? Maybe it doesn't matter. But maybe you will miss opportunities and threats and, worst of all, maybe you will begin to convince yourself that yours is the best way. Even the only way. To consider those who have not discovered your way to be unfortunate. Again, along with the others with the same beam setting, you get into "group think."

David Simon uses the same analogy: *"You must have your radar screen set broad. Then you will hear about the problems and opportunities before they hit you. You will also spot the white noise – the noise that is put out to confuse you when you read your screen. You must not delegate the patrolling of the outer reaches of the screen to others, you have to do it yourself. Dangerous leaders aren't hearing the bleeps from out there. And then they have to make the really tough calls on the strange blips – and they make huge mistakes. Sometimes the mistakes are about people, but most often they are about events."* He gave an example of the effects of closed networks and narrow radar. Think of the Maginot Line: the defensive system that the French spent vast amounts of money and effort building after the First World War, because they feared another German invasion. The enormous fortifications, stretching hundreds of miles, took years to build. The planners simply did not see that warfare was going to be different and that, in future, it would be about mobility, not entrenchment.

Good radar helps you distinguish between what matters and what doesn't, and see where the problems and opportunities are going to come from. It also helps you decide your timing. You need to be listening to the bleeps all the time, especially noting when they change. Malvinder Singh is Chief Executive of Ranbaxy in India. He says: "*As a leader, I think you have to be picking up the early warning systems in the ever changing, and ever faster changing, global environment. Only then you will be able to keep ahead and avoid being dragged by the market.*"

If you need convincing of the importance of networks, talk to someone who does not have them. Dr Musharraf Hussain says: "*The Muslim community in Britain does not put enough effort into this. Maybe, as a minority, you are tempted to revert to your own space. It's almost a ghetto mentality. But it is hard to build the networks. If you don't understand enough about how power works, you are unclear about who to influence, who to develop relationships with, and who to target. It all feels unfamiliar. There are no trusted guides. Then competing priorities mean that you don't think you can justify many meetings with no apparent outcome other than building contacts, and so you don't meet new people.*" And you become ever more isolated.

Last word on this to Sandy Forrest: "*You need networks because you can never tell who will prove to be really useful in five or ten years time. But networking is not about using people. It is about sharing with people so that they see as much benefit from the relationship as you do. Don't be a networking tart: it is not about being able to approach someone and remind them you have already met. It is about them wanting to approach you.*"

So creating networks is important. As is developing them and nurturing them. And the skills required to lead a network are the same as the skills required to lead beyond authority: because, in a network, there is no authority other than that which the members of it choose to volunteer.

IT'S ABOUT PEOPLE 3: DIVERSITY

Diversity is creativity

If people sneer at the word "networks," they are certainly tired of "diversity." Some see it merely as a legal tripwire designed to prevent them from doing things. Others are sick of the platitudes and the carefully drafted and crafted statements of commitment. Quite apart from the moral issues about discrimination, I see diversity as creativity. Save me from teams of people who agree with each other. They are stale and unexciting. We did an assessment of the impact of Common Purpose programs on leaders. It showed that most people came away determined never to work in a homogeneous team again. Of course, they had experienced tensions and the time it took to work them through. But they had also seen how exciting and energizing it is when people of every possible kind of diversity get together.

We have leaders on the programs from every sector, background, race, creed, sexuality, and set of beliefs, every political place and conviction, able-bodied and disabled, tall and short, fat and thin. Real diversity. The ideas flow and the mix reveals worries and angles and connections and opportunities. Many have never seen or experienced this before. I love this – it makes all the long years on trains and planes worthwhile. If we have 20,000 graduates of the UK programs and an ever-growing number internationally, then we have created glorious converts to real diversity and the creativity it releases.

New angles

Diverse teams tend to spot new angles faster. This is what really excites leaders in the outer circles. It is best expressed by David Simon: *"I was at a board meeting the day after the Berlin Wall came down. We did the business fast and spent five hours thinking through what we thought this would mean for Germany. It was a fascinating discussion among 14 very powerful people, all very well-informed thinkers. Only one got it right: the trade union official, who said it would mean 15 to 20 years of hard labor for Germany. All the others were thinking at the geopolitical level. He thought about the cultural gap at the working level. That's what you need diversity for."* Apparently, General Patton once said: *"If they are all thinking alike, then someone is not thinking."* He was right. But maybe it wasn't just that they were switched off and thinking alike. Maybe he didn't have a diverse team around him to start with.

I remember an Eritrean businessman who came on the Common Purpose program in West London. He was chair of the local Eritrean refugee group and had been surprised by many things as he had learnt alongside fellow Londoners who were certainly not as bad as he had been led to believe. There were very few on his radar, so he had been relying on the accounts of others. At the end of the program, he said: *"We do not have any people who are not Eritreans on our board. We should, shouldn't we?"* I agreed. *"Because, if we are about helping Eritreans to become part of West London, we should."* Again, yes. *"Do you think anyone who was not Eritrean would do it?"* Yes. So he went away and asked two new members to join (inviting just one would have been unkind and put the person into too much of a minority position). And it became not just an Eritrean community group, but an Eritrean community group in West London.

Seeing through other people's eyes

If, as leaders in the first outer circle, we are going to work across our organizations so that they are ever more effective, getting the geeks to work with the creeps (or whatever they are currently calling each other), we need to be in pretty regular contact with both the geeks and the creeps and understand where they are coming from. If, as leaders in the second outer circle, we are to counter the forces of fragmentation that we see all around us in society (as leaders form views on just about every social issue based on limited networks, compounded by what they read and watch), then we need to get better at seeing other people's perspectives. We need to switch up the radar setting – and fast. We need to learn to overcome the panic. To counter the overwhelming urge to step backwards when we meet someone strange, rather than take a step forwards because we recognize an opportunity to see things through their eyes.

Sometimes the other perspectives are hard to swallow. Chris Mathias was telling me how the UK felt to him when he first arrived: *"The British are warlike. Look at our politics, our courts, our parliament. In fact, look at our roads. Congestion in India is 5,000 times worse, but you don't see road rage. Maybe it comes from being an island. And the British are cold too – just watch most British men dance. I consider it a great compliment now when I break through this coldness. When you arrive in Britain, you have to learn many different ways. For example, you have to learn rapidly that eye-contact amongst strangers is not accepted."* I still haven't decided on all this. It is hard to accept what other people say about your own reality (and my husband dances well). I don't know if Chris is right, but thinking it through helps (it certainly helps me to understand Chris). It was harder hearing Tarek Ben Halim: *"I have a lot of respect for Britain and the British and I know that my children will be welcomed here and people will fight for their right to be here and to be treated properly. But I also know that they will never be allowed to belong. And the trouble is that even the people who clearly regard themselves as (and indeed often are) the most tolerant are those who are very clear that you don't belong."* I went home a bit stunned and sad, thinking about our long history as an island – one that I am very proud of, having seen and experienced alongside friends some of the crude racism of other parts of Europe. I went to bed thinking of my colleague Sue Crawford's cooking. It's a combination of Caribbean and British, two cultures that have merged and produced far more delicious food.

Maybe you just have to have the grace to accept things that are said to you in good faith. You don't have to agree with them but, having listened, at least you will be more likely to understand – and you will be more effective as you work together. David Bell talks about diversity of generations: *"I remember reading about Saint Benedict. He said that you must always listen to the young monks because they remember the things that you have forgotten."* Indeed, when you listen to the young now, wherever you are, you are struck by how complex and multiple their identities are. Unlike David Bell, who probably sees himself as one thing – British – they have three, four, or even five identities and sets of loyalties (British and Muslim and Pakistani, for example) and they don't find this strange or conflicting or even difficult, just the way it is.

Listen to the young, the old, everyone, says David Varney, and you can learn a lot: *"At O₂, we needed to look at the diversity of our workforce. I remember meeting a group of women staff who had good suggestions and so did the African Caribbean group. But it was the Asian group that were really clever. They came in with a presentation on how to get more of the Asian market for O₂. They said that we didn't have a big enough share of this customer base and made a series of suggestions about how to get it."*

Be an outsider

To really enjoy diversity and bring out the creativity it generates and get the perspectives it brings, I think a profound interest in people helps. But perhaps it helps too if, as Jude Kelly says: *"You have been an outsider yourself. You need outsiders – but you work with them better if you have been there too."*

A while ago, my husband returned from a business trip to Japan. He loves walking around cities watching things and, after the very polite and formal friendliness of the day, he went for a walk in the evening. As he walked around the streets, he experienced racism against himself for the first time. He walked into a bar and asked for a drink, only to be told that it would cost him $400. Stunned, he turned and people jeered as he left. He is big and strong and well-educated and white. It was quite a shock to realize that nothing he could say or do would change their view of him. Everything that in the UK sends the message that he belongs had the opposite effect in Japanese streets.

Pam Chesters saw things very differently when she was on the Race Equality Council in Camden in north London years ago: *"Having been a senior woman in the oil industry, I was used to being in a minority, but my experience of being in a minority within the context of race was a new one. As someone brought up in Edinburgh, educated at St. Andrews, and working for BP, I had very few friends who were black. When I moved to Camden and was elected to the Council, this obviously changed. I became one of the Council nominees on the local Race Equality Council. At times, there were some tense moments – when the REC needed to support the minority communities who felt victimized, essentially by the white community. It didn't always seem that way from my perspective, which was sometimes a bit uncomfortable, but I could see from their point of view why they felt this. It taught me to see their experience in a whole different light."*

Many years ago, I made a speech at a conference about industrial relations. As I got going, about 15 people pointedly walked out. A fellow speaker whispered: *"Keep going, they just don't like women."* This is the only time I have ever experienced really crude in-your-face sexism. It was a long time ago but very formative. I have bottled the disgust and fear and rage and the feeling of not being good enough. And I use it to understand others. Especially when you are operating in the outer circles and need to work across so many different worlds, engaging as much talent as you can. Because there is not enough talent in the world to squander it: female, or black, or disabled, or Eritrean (or white, for that matter).

Maybe I am just impatient and need to take a longer-term view. As

Doug Miller says: "*When you consider the arguments about diversity, it is worth remembering that, when the Equal Opportunities Act was introduced in the USA 30 years ago, there were Harvard professors saying that, because women had less experience of team sports, they would be less effective at leadership because they would not know how to build teams.*"

Political correctness

The accusation that some viewpoint or rule is based on political correctness has become a bit of a catch-all over the years. For some, it has become a way of writing off or rubbishing things that feel very strange and unfamiliar (particularly in the outermost circles) without having to take the time to understand them.

Think of all those leaders who refused point blank to fill in equal opportunities forms. The forms seemed alien; to some, quite offensive. But if you sit down and talk through how we propose to hand on a more cohesive society to our children, I think you begin to persuade them that we have to have diversity on the boards of the public bodies. If there is some logic in this case, if we are to produce change over time, we need to track progress. Which means we need information about the processes of making appointments now. Which is why they need to fill in the equal opportunities forms. It is not "political correctness" – it is logical.

Peter Sherratt says we have to get on with this because, quite simply: "*Diversity plays a big role in risk management. It produces the checks and balances. If you have a team of all men or all women, you simply don't spot all the pitfalls.*" I think there is another problem: all-white and male boards look so complacent in the modern world. So divorced from reality. I do not understand why organizations choose to send out this message about their brand.

There is no need to appoint inexperienced or unqualified applicants. Mainly it is about taking the time to find able candidates and persuade them to apply. Because many have become pretty sick of adorning short lists to make them look more diverse, knowing full well that they will never be appointed.

Gone mad – or just too far?

This is not to say that the criticism has no validity at all. As Pam Chesters says: "*The political correctness that is most irritating is when a statement is made, not by the minority on whose behalf it is being argued, but by other self-appointed individuals who take it upon themselves to argue a particular point without checking whether it is a genuine problem. For example, people who go on about getting rid of Christmas celebrations in schools so as not to offend those of other religions. Personally, I have never met anyone of another faith who is not relaxed about this – quite rightly, we celebrate a number of festivals of other religions in schools anyway."*

Bharat Mehta agrees wholeheartedly. But he also returns to the issue of writing off what is unfamiliar: *"Leaders have a tendency to dismiss things that are outside their realm. In the old days, you had the expression 'loony left,' and with it you threw out both the good and the bad. Basically, you were dismissing anything you did not comprehend with throw-away lines."*

There is a powerful warning in this. As Zenna Atkins says: *"The expression 'political correctness' is becoming a menace. It is in danger of undermining very real and legitimate concerns about offensive and unpleasant attitudes. These are creeping back in, and people are becoming afraid to challenge for fear of appearing to be politically correct."*

Experience diversity

How do you get better at understanding diversity? So that you feel comfortable enough about difference to be able to tempt people from diverse backgrounds to work with you? So that diversity becomes a strength, rather than a weakness? A source of creativity and ideas? You do it by endlessly putting yourself in situations where you are in a minority. Volunteer to join the board of an Eritrean community group if you have little experience of racial discrimination. Or join a program alongside white London leaders if you are Eritrean.

Reflecting back, I realize that I started with a huge advantage. The place where for the longest period of my childhood we stayed in one place was Manhattan, New York. Though, at the time, an utterly miserable place to bring up a child, it was a good place to be if you wanted to understand what has now become known as diversity. Well, less to understand it, more to live it. I went to the French Lycée there and my classroom had every kind of person in it. The children of the French Ambassador to the United Nations and of the waiter at the French bistro on the corner. Kids from the Ivory Coast and Senegal. Many children whose grandparents had walked across Europe with all they possessed on their backs. Christians, Muslims, and Jews, though I had (and have) no idea who was which. I remember hearing, years later, that a childhood friend had become the editor of *The Jewish Chronicle* and I was surprised that they would appoint someone who was not a Jew, until it occurred to me that he was. Everyone was different, so you never really bothered to find out about the differences. In my teenage years, masses of kids arrived from the Lebanon. There was always change and difference. I think I was blissfully unaware of prejudice – which must have been all around me – as we lived in Harlem. As a result, I don't see difference and don't start to figure people out the minute I meet them, based on how they speak or look.

Know your blind spots

We all have blind spots and we need to know them. I have them. I've acquired them both consciously and unconsciously. I try to keep learning by putting myself into new situations where I will see things from other angles. And, even better, keep experiencing what it feels like to be in a minority. I know that I will never be as British as I was in New York. As a member of a minority, I became a very strident one, and would not hear a word said against the UK. I have changed a bit since then.

In my non-executive roles, I was a founding trustee of Demos, a cross-party independent think tank where I was the only non-hugely-intelligent-academically-brilliant one. It was good for me, because I have always been prejudiced against intellectuals.

As a trustee of the Windsor Fellowships, a charity led by black people to develop young black high flyers, I saw race issues in London from another angle. On the board of Impetus Trust (a group of venture capitalists introducing venture philanthropy to the UK) I am the only "low net worth" trustee, and I have learnt about financing and seen the world from a business operator's angle.

I have also been an independent assessor of public appointments, working with the civil servants and ministers as they selected people to fill public positions. My role was to ensure that proper process was followed (basically, that politicians didn't just appoint their best friends). As I had been critical over the years of the appointments process, the challenge was to try to be part of changing it. In truth, the experience only really confirmed my prejudices.

Then I became a trustee of the Arab Learning Initiative. Working with Tarek Ben Halim, I discovered that I knew little about the Arab world. And much of what I thought I knew was refracted through an entire childhood in the French educational system. As a result, although I have managed to avoid most of the British forms of racism (the minorities in the UK tend to be from the Indian sub-continent), I had always felt uncomfortable about the Arab world. As a result of more recent experience, this feeling has now gone. But it taught me that you have to watch out for your prejudices – especially ones you hardly know you have.

All these roles have taught me a lot. Not least about how badly I can behave when I am in the minority. But, over the years, I have become better – and more effective. As a result, I have also learnt to help others to join groups in which they are in the minority.

SCENARIO: STRUGGLING WITH DIVERSITY

The word "diversity" is appearing more and more. How do you deal with the difficult (and often quite private) issues the term evokes?

Dame Jane Campbell is an independent social policy adviser at the Department of Health and former Chair of the Social Care Institute for Excellence.

I am pretty tired of the word diversity and of all the words that surround it. I am especially sick, for example, of the word "vulnerable." People use it in a very disempowering way. To be described as a vulnerable person immediately makes one a victim and portrays one in a very ineffectual way. It is not the person who is innately vulnerable but the (vulnerable) situation they find themselves in. So, for instance, I am vulnerable when I do not receive funding for the personal assistant who gets me out of bed for work; if I do not have accessible housing or transport and I am forced to negotiate an inaccessible environment. If these needs are met, I am as strong and capable as any of my non-disabled peers. We then have a level playing field. No one has the right to stereotype us as vulnerable people. No one can put themselves in a disabled person's shoes. You don't know what it's like until you have been left on the toilet or on the floor because your assistant has wandered off or not turned up for work. That's what makes me vulnerable, not the fact that I cannot walk or feed myself."

Kuben Naidoo is Head of Fiscal Policy at the Treasury in South Africa.

It was late in 1988, at the national conference of the South African Youth Congress held in the beautiful town of KaNyamazane, when I first heard a delegate from the Western Cape call for "affirmative action." The crowd went wild. I nudged the comrade next to me: "Hey, what's affirmative action?" He said it means "positive discrimination." I thought about it for a minute. This struck fear into me. That discrimination was a bad thing was ingrained in me from childhood. Were we going to do the same thing as the apartheid government? Since then, I have discovered that affirmative action has a number of downsides. With the best will in the world, it will always leave an emotional or psychological effect on people: both the beneficiaries and those who were historically privileged.

The beneficiaries are often placed in a terrible position where their colleagues doubt their abilities. Sometimes they doubt their own abilities and wonder whether their promotion was because of their potential to do the job, or because the company has to meet certain quotas. This type of psychological trauma is damaging to our long-term ability to develop smart, confident young leaders.

Many young white people suffer from emotional trauma too. They feel that their talents are not wanted in the country of their birth, that they are victims of some type of revenge for the sins of apartheid. How do we build a country, a united people, when a significant minority feel that they are not valued? Most young white South Africans want to contribute towards the development of a new South Africa. Many recognize the ill effects of apartheid, and the only way that they can contribute towards its eradication is through staying and working and paying their taxes.

Despite these criticisms of affirmative action, I am unequivocally in favor of it. Let me explain why.

It is naïve to think that, in a rapid growing economy, the legacy of apartheid can be reversed merely by improving the education and training system. Yes, we must improve the education system. However, on its own, this will not substantially change the demographics of the workplace and of the boardroom. The human capital, the social infrastructure, built up over generations of privilege for white South Africans, cannot be equaled by simply fixing schooling.

Educationists believe that two-thirds of the deductive or reasoning ability of children is formed before they start school. The factors that affect their development include: whether the parents can read, the presence of books and newspapers, the presence of a television, a stimulating play area, nutrition, and diet. All of these factors are outside the ambit of the public schooling system. The education system would have to perform exceptionally well to level the playing field. Many middle-class people think that they are well off because they worked hard in school, that their parents worked hard to educate them and, implicitly, if anyone else has less education, then they were lazy in school. This is a myth. Social capital, built up over generations, transferred from parent to child, is one of the biggest explanatory factors affecting economic development and well-being. These things can be turned around, but they require monumental effort – and time.

If, in 20 years' time, all the rich people are mainly white and all the poor people are mainly black, the sustainability of South Africa's democracy would surely come into question. The development of a large black middle class is absolutely essential for the functioning of democracy. It is in the long-term interest of white South Africans, and the owners of capital, that we aggressively change the color of the workplace and boardroom. Affirmative action is one of the tools that should be used to grow this middle class. It just will not happen without it.

Inequality is a bad thing. If that inequality continues to be defined on racial terms, then it would be even easier for some populist to come along, whip up support, get elected, and put short-term, get-rich-quick schemes at the front of government policy. This would be the Mugabe option. Short-termism would rule – and the prospects of building a sustainable, prosperous, non-racial democracy on the southern tip of Africa would come tumbling down.

To those who have their doubts about affirmative action, I wish to say that the ills of the past are too deep rooted to be changed automatically through the normal course of events, even in a rapidly growing economy. We must focus on the long term: the achievement of a society where discrimination is bad, no matter what. We are not yet there. We must recognize that.

But, at the same time, those of us who support affirmative action must be mindful of the emotional and psychological damage that it does, on all sides. We must be constantly aware that affirmative action creates uncomfortable and sometimes unnecessary tension in the society, making it more difficult to forge a united nation.

Zenna Atkins is Chair of Places for People.

One of the great problems in Britain today is that we are all trying to become the same: to minimize the differences between us, rather than enjoy them. I am a tall busty blonde. I like being a tall busty blonde. I flaunt it – mainly because there are not many of us chairing boards (particularly not the audit committee of the Royal Navy). It's me. I add value precisely because I am different. Because I think, talk, and look different. I don't want to hide my difference. I feel comfortable with diversity – I like it. Of course, it is very alienating to walk into a room and be the only person who looks like you. The temptation is to dress "as one might" and think that, if you want to excel in a white man's world, you have to be as much like a white man as you can. I think it is sad to see how many people do follow this line and compromise and change. I feel this pressure too – but nevertheless I usually wear my lowest-cut tops and highest-heeled shoes for my Navy work. They appointed me because I would challenge the stereotype – and I do. Somehow, I think we need to resist the temptation to become the same.

It is very sad that, here we are in the twenty-first century, in an affluent and prosperous country, and we still stumble around these issues. Nowhere is this more evident than on boards and in senior teams where, all too often, people look alike, think alike, and say the same things. The NHS Appointments Commission was set up some three years ago to attract a greater range of people to NHS boards. There was justified concern that the members were all knights of the realm (or married to them), or retired military dignitaries (or married to them). Three years on, the Commission has just appointed nine of the ten new Strategic Health Authority chairs. We have eight knights, two dignitaries, and one woman (I do not know who she is married to).

We are bad on diversity because very few people feel comfortable with it. The majority fall into two camps: those who are inherently prejudiced and want things to be "like they used to be" (most of them have just about managed to stop themselves from saying this out loud); and those who think things should be different, but feel very uncomfortable about exactly what to do about it. Mostly, they set up rules to help them feel better. These rules, often called "diversity policies," are used to prove that they (or their organizations) are not prejudiced, because they stick to them by the letter. But nothing actually changes.

When you recognize the value of diversity, it no longer becomes an option to keep recruiting or promoting within the mold. However much the public sector squirms at terms like "institutional racism," the fact that their management and governance structures are predominantly white means that they cannot be providing services that allow people of color to feel comfortable, empathized with, and accepted. I love being different when I am on the board of an organization. But if you are a customer, and you don't have power, it is not at all liberating or fun to be different. It is demoralizing and difficult.

THE RIGHT METHOD 1: STRATEGY

Working the systems

Beyond your authority, you have to be clever. Not just intellectually – but strategically. You have to know that every system is different. In fact, assume it is and look forward to the difference. Then you won't underestimate the difference and be wrong-footed. Each time you take on something new, you need to recognize that power works in different ways there. You need to get to know the new system and then work it. There are some common threads on strategy. For Paddy Ashdown, it's the ability to *"build coalitions and conspire."* I would add the ability to work the right relationships with authority – whatever the authority is in any situation.

Building coalitions

The ability to build coalitions is a basic requirement. First you need to understand how important they are. Then you need the will to actually build them. Paddy Ashdown says it's the lack of this will that makes most businessmen incapable of leading beyond their authority: *" They don't have the patience to build coalitions. They simply won't make the endless compromises."* If you don't want all the faff involved, then stay in your core circle. Because coalitions take time. They are messy. And, if you are used to straightforward power, they can be extremely frustrating. Listen to Vince McGinlay about his days leading beyond authority at M&S: *"It was horrible! Having to go to essentially the same meeting time and time again. Always looking at the same issues, just packaged differently. It was five years of frustration. Of almost never making the final decisions. Of making the case, making it compelling, but never getting to tick the box."*

But if you can build coalitions, it's worth it. And not just in the outer circles either. As Ned Sullivan says: *"Every corporation in the world is run by a chief executive who wants to expand their people's thinking so that they operate in formal and informal ways beyond their circle of authority. Those that do are listened to. They are coalition builders. They have learnt to build bridges and form alliances amongst all the 'no people' who can prevent them from having an impact. In the outer circle, you can't just have chief executives operating on their own – you need the coalition builders to bring along the 'no people.' It's a long and exhausting process and not all leaders will want to do it, or be successful at it."*

Reflecting on coalition builders he has come across, Ned says that they are leaders who are always carefully prepared for the issues that difficult people will raise. They always put aside time and energy to drop in on colleagues. They know all the secretaries well. They seldom make hasty decisions – and they never give instructions. Amy Fawcett would add that they are always prepared to listen: "*The trouble is that, if you think you are fantastic, if you think you have all the answers, you tend not to listen. I wonder whether some of the most successful business leaders who came over from the USA to Europe in the 1980s to a new market for them and built successful businesses, were in fact successful because they were more open and receptive? Maybe if you think you have all the answers, you are less likely to listen to and learn from others, and therefore less likely to be able to build something better out of the amalgamation of the best, wherever it comes from.*"

Coalitions cannot be built by people who think that the only way to the top is to fight off others who are also trying to get there. Or by leaders who spend their time beating off challenges to their own success. Or who think that their role is to pour boiling water over the people below them. To be a coalition builder, you need to believe in teams.

Derek Higgs carried out his review of corporate governance as an individual, not as part of a group. It's a fine call sometimes whether to go for a committee or a single person. A committee will provide strength in numbers and diversity of views, but can slow you down. The individual approach can leave you personally vulnerable, no matter how thorough the supporting research and consultation. As Derek says: "*I had the benefit of the views of a diverse group of leaders from industry and the City. They were outspoken, they didn't always agree amongst themselves or with me, they were hugely valuable, and they were never publicly identified. It speeded up the process, but there were times when I wondered whether a committee up there alongside me might not have been preferable.*"

The guiding coalition

I first heard this phrase from Moira Wallace, who believes in the benefit of coalitions in building the foundations of any successful initiative which aims to create change: "*I agree with those people who say that, for change to work, you need a guiding coalition: a group of people who help you articulate why the change is necessary, and who are prepared to put a small amount of their time into helping it happen. They contribute advice, they tell you if you're going wrong, they prepare the way for the change, and they enlist others. When you go about producing change, you need to think through who is going to help – and gather them. Then, as you proceed, you need to keep checking in with them. Beware going into a darkened room and trying to do it all yourself."*

If you are going to lead a coalition, you need to know how to craft a guiding coalition first. So you need to be well enough networked to know who to draw in – and how.

I find this idea very helpful. I think of the various things I have started or helped others to start. First finding the friends, the helpers, the doubtful but useful, the crucial. Working out how to draw them all in. Then going to see them with the ideas, and slowly tempting them and flattering and inspiring them in. Before you know it, it's no longer "I" but "we." I did this to Prue Leith a while ago – and she was on to me. She kept interrupting and teasing me as she watched me try to enroll her into a new venture. She was always one step ahead of me. But, in the end, I still got her inadvertently to sit forward and say: *"But how are we going to do that?"* She said "we." I had her – and she knew it. Then, as the coalition grows, others bring more people to the party. Slowly, with their guidance, you get clever at figuring out where all the constituencies are and how to deal with each one.

Consensus by another name?

For some people, the word coalition means consensus – and that means compromise. They imagine they would end up with a miserable, watered down solution because they couldn't get everyone to commit to a brave one. Yet many really effective coalitions are comprised of people who are not interested in consensus. They are only interested in what works. David Puttnam explains the difference: *"Coalitions are modern; consensus is the old way. With coalitions, you are getting a group of people to agree on an objective (if they won't, it's not a coalition) but to park some of their disagreements about how to deliver on it as they work together. With a consensus, you require agreement not just on the objectives but on every step of the way, on the means too. There is no place to park the disagreement in a consensus. In the UK, we are not naturally that good at producing coalitions because we are so used to either losing or winning, even if there is only one vote in it."*

Study the galaxy

When you're planning a coalition, it may be helpful to use a model that has served us well at Common Purpose when doing development work in a new area, whether it be Teesside or Istanbul, Bangalore or Hamburg. We use the vocabulary of outer space (though I cannot vouch for its astronomical accuracy). And I think it is a very useful shorthand which helps to analyze sources of power: suns, stars, moons, shooting stars, and black holes.

Suns are people who shine the brightest: their rays light up and warm others. Stars are potential future suns: they are on their way, but their light and warmth is not yet as strong. Moons are often wonderful – but they are on their way out. Shooting stars are people who look deceptively bright and exciting but they will fade and, when they do, they are dangerous. Black holes are wasters of energy: where you can put an awful lot of time to no great effect (they also suck the power from others).

In any organization or community, all these bodies will be present. But you need to be able to recognize them – and distinguish between them. Suns you need: having them will make everything so much easier. Stars you need too: for now and the future. Moons you can easily misidentify: they're attractive and you can admire them and be drawn to them (you may even be egged on by them), but they can't help you when the going gets tough because they have very little power left. With their nostalgia for an entity they used to know (or, worse still, regret the passing of) they may well encourage you in the wrong direction. Shooting stars could be useful: but they may not keep going for long enough. Black holes cannot be ignored or discounted: they are often in crucial positions – but you can put too much time and energy into them for very little return.

In a city, for example, the chief executive of the hospital and a businessman may be suns. To start Common Purpose there, we need the suns to be either onside or happy to let it happen. There can be stars everywhere: they may be running companies or community groups or organizations of all sorts, or they might be lone campaigners. We need a decent proportion of them, from across all the sectors.

A moon might be the chief executive of the development company that is on its way out. She was hugely important, but is now thinking about the next job and has got pretty bitter about the people who got in her way in the company. She might be incredibly kind and generous and give you a false sense of support (false because she is not in a position to deliver on it). A shooting star might be an entrepreneur whose business is starting to go wrong. And the black holes, like the stars, could be anywhere: they are very powerful, but it's only negative power. They will oppose change because it is inconvenient or will show them up.

Over time, the map of the galaxy changes. People move from being black holes to stars and even suns. Others take their place. People come and go, as agendas and priorities change. So you need to keep the telescope trained on the sky. I have sat with many friends talking through who they need to draw into their coalitions. And whether they are right to want them, just in case they are being led on by a shooting star or seduced by a moon.

Conspiracy: some theories

So what of conspiring? The "dark arts"? As Simon Fanshawe says: *"You have to be honest about the dark arts. I don't mean doing things that are unethical or illegal; merely that, sometimes, you have to count the votes, persuade politically rather than with the beauty of rational argument."*

Prue Leith calls it skullduggery: *"You have to be very clever to overcome the jealousies and the instincts to destroy, which are deep. You have to listen hard, schmooze a lot, pretend everyone is on board, use flattery and the sweetest of bribery."*

I know that in Downing Street they are always wondering whether people have sufficient "guile" to be brought into a coalition the government is building.

Doug Miller, with his military background, clarifies it further: *"You start with clear and defined objectives. This is the most important. Military training teaches you to understand this. Then you establish what the obstacles are. They could be structural or financial, but they are usually people. So you have to establish what motivates them, and then decide if you can win them over by the power of the idea, or by finding a fit where you can align both of your interests. If not, you look to form alliances, or to make compromises. Sometimes, if it gets messy, you might have to run over them, undermine them, go around them, or discredit them. As a last resort, you consider bullying them, or buying them off, but this is usually when you are getting close to victory, and they are trying to minimize their losses."*

Remember Brandon Gough: *"How do you isolate people who are stopping progress? First, intellectually, by showing them that they are not on strong ground. Second, you have to persuade other people to stand up to the blocker, to show that the price of doing so is not too high, or that the blocker and their allies will back off if resisted with conviction."*

You have to watch the people who ultimately won't go with your coalition, who are blockers – and I mean real blockers. I remember watching a colleague who was dealing with a group who were simmering, just waiting to double-cross him, and both he and they knew it. He stated very clearly, but without ever actually taking anybody on, *"I know you wouldn't for a moment consider undermining my trust by doing ..."* The other guys had got the point loud and clear.

Andrew Cubie says that neutralizing the opposition sometimes just comes down to *"he who blinks first."* It's a dare. Whatever the game – poker, chess, pool, backgammon – you have to keep something up your sleeve. Let's face it, every organization has its way of neutralizing behavior it does not like, so you need to play a careful game.

Conspiring can only be entered into with the objective clearly in mind. And be careful that others may be better at it than you – and are conspiring too. A friend tells me: *"If you are going to deal with the center of any government, you need to read a John Le Carré book every night. Be most fearful when they are at their most charming."* And, from another far too well-informed source: *"It's more like what you think China was like under Mao than anyone imagines. The closed doors, the whispering, the treachery."* I don't think this is just about governments either. Many organizations – large and small – have these characteristics too.

Setting up useful idiots

I spoke to another friend recently who described how she had set someone up. Using all her charm and flattery, she had drawn him in and then installed him as a convenient useful idiot. (This is someone, I might add, who is far from being a useful idiot in all the other things he does). My friend's intention was to get him to produce a report which she knew full well would be a perfect smokescreen for her own activities. While all the "no people" and the opposers fought him and his work and his developing ideas, she would quietly slide though half the changes she was sure he was going to suggest. Everyone would be delighted with her achievements *"when it could have been so much worse."* Ask the useful idiot himself and he will tell you how incredibly helpful and supportive my friend had been while he battled with the constituencies.

Have I ever done this? Yes. I think of the boards I have been on over the years where there were people demanding action. Where, as a board, we have known that there were bigger and more pressing priorities to address, but that we had to be seen to be hearing the cries. It was certainly useful to produce the distraction of creating a sub-committee, led by someone who did not really understand the big picture, to look into an issue in depth, with no timetable, so that we could get on with what we saw as the important issues.

I don't think I have ever set up a useful idiot because I knew that there was something important to deal with, and I did not have the courage or time or brains or energy to do it. Even though I knew that I should. But I can think of moments, reading the papers and hearing about the creation of a government inquiry into an issue or event, when I have thought: "Clever them. They have put in a useful (enthusiastic, genuine, slightly misguided, sometimes very grand) useful idiot while they get on with their own agenda or avoid dealing with one that might cause difficulties ahead."

I can also think of important issues that have needed to be addressed where, because there was an existing body apparently on the case, momentum was halted and nothing happened. The existing initiative might have got out of date or discredited or simply tired, somehow beginning to lose the plot but refusing to hand on the baton, and by its presence, prevents others from taking up the issue. These are sometimes very sad stories in the campaigning world, where the original initiative started as brave and bold and difficult and effective, but the struggle to survive, to gain funds, to keep up the energy, to prove impact, becomes exhausting and very slowly (and sadly – and dangerously) it becomes part of the problem, because it prevents something else from happening. I spoke to a British foundation, which hands out funds in huge amounts in the UK, about such a story. For many years, they had sponsored an organization that was now on the brink of falling into this trap. It had been a great initiative that was addressing a huge problem of the day, holding a torch through many decades when no one else was brave enough even to discuss the issue. The foundation had funded it through thick and thin, as the great funders do. Considering this year's application, they knew full well that it was now on the point of fulfilling the role of useful idiot. But to abandon it after so many years, hard long years, was almost impossible to envisage.

Gather your intelligence

If you are going down the conspiring route, Sandy Forrest says, make sure you have great intelligence: "*Knowledge is power, so you need to try to acquire as much of other people's knowledge as you can. It's intelligence gathering. You slowly build up a picture, a jigsaw, as you piece its bits together. You increasingly come to the situation where the partly completed jigsaw enables you to gain confidence in your discussions with people. Then you really start to make progress. At some stages, you bluff. You pretend to know more than you do because people (even people who won't generally break confidences) are happy to discuss issues in detail if they believe that you already know as much, if not more, than they do. When the picture is complete, you are probably the only person who can see it in full. Others have only their bits to work on. Now you can give other people the bits they are missing and a sense of the whole, and this will help them to make sense of the bits they already have. At the end, when the outcome is known, you will be congratulated for your insight. In fact, it was just good intelligence gathering.*"

Working with authority

You also need to make sure you know where the authority is in different situations. Have you got this right – or are you chasing after a moon and thinking it's a sun? Especially in the outer circles, people don't understand what the unfamiliar system is well enough to spot where the authority really is. And you need to make sure you understand different kinds of authority. I remember hearing a woman whose experience, to date, had only been with appointed leaders. She was now working with elected leaders and had discovered to what extent they have to play a very different game. Not, as she had thought, an entirely duplicitous one, but a very different one. It comes back to the pilot in his plane: you need to understand the workings well enough to know which buttons to press and which ones to avoid – and to know that different planes have different systems.

Once you know who the authority is, you have to figure out how to deal with it. Whether, in this case, you need to be a rebel or a transformer. If you don't get your relationship with authority right, you can end up being such an outsider that you can't even be an effective rebel. And, if you don't spend time sorting it out, you can easily fall into the "useful idiot" role.

Gill Morgan is one of the most effective leaders beyond her authority

I have ever met. In addition to her "theory of goodness," she has an excellent way to describe how you deal with an unbalanced relationship with power, when you're David to someone else's Goliath: *"Most of the time, you must be the influencer from the inside. Maybe 95 percent. Only 5 percent can be as an outsider, when you speak out, and it's usually because it looks like you won't win. If you do it too often, people will lose trust. I work on a" pennies from heaven" basis. You have to store up your pennies. You do favors, and give views, and take on tasks others will not touch, and build coalitions and provide information, and back down on some issues that don't matter that much. In so doing, you build up a whole store of pennies. And then, when you need something that really matters, you can draw them down. For every 10 to 20 pennies I put in, I can only draw one down. You have to be very careful you draw them down on the right issues. You know that the deal is imbalanced. Because those in authority always want – and will get – more. And you know the rebels think you are a terrible compromiser. But you know quietly (because no one else is likely to) that it's the right deal and that you achieve the objective best this way."*

When he was Managing Director of Twin Trading, Albert Tucker was a free-trade pioneer. He perhaps had to fight authority even harder than most. It is not an easy ride. He would add that, when you are dealing with authority and you know that this time you actually have to square up and fight, you need the same advice he gives the kids' football team he trains: *"You have to meet the other side with equal determination, otherwise you will get flattened or injured. You certainly won't win."*

What will knock you off course

So you need strategy. But you also need to be able to grasp opportunities as they present themselves. I love the phrase: "strategic opportunist." Maybe this is what you really have to be in the outer circles. But, in your opportunism, beware of what might knock you off course.

Lack of resolve

If you don't set off with enough determination and self-belief you will come unstuck, come what may. You have to muster an enormous amount of determination because you are in unfamiliar territory. Chris Mathias tells a story about a small plane that went down in the Andes. A group of desperate survivors huddled together in the middle of the jungle trying to figure out how to survive. One man stood up, held up his map and said: "Follow me." They did – and he led them to safety. It was only as they were recovering that they found out that the map was not of the Andes but of the Alps. As Chris says, even if you are not quite sure of your best course, sometimes you need to set off with total confidence, because that is the only option – even if you cannot plot it all out.

Too much information

My father believed that there was almost no situation in life that could not be made infinitely worse with a thorough explanation. When I was pregnant for the first time, my mother bought me a book about maternity. It was cleverly set out: each spread showed what would happen in each of the 40 weeks. I was absolutely clear that I would only ever read about the week I was in. Because I knew that, if I read ahead and discovered what was coming my way, I would have abandoned all hope. I am now also clear that, if there had been a second book about the teenage years, I would have been even worse. Better to have a clear idea of the objective, a wonderful baby in 40 weeks, maybe even some milestones (scans and the like), but certainly not the detail. Some planning is called for. But if you plot it all out, you may never do it.

Diversions and distractions

It's easy to allow yourself to be distracted from the objective. As John Inge says, you mustn't be put off by the orange squash: *"You have to keep reminding yourself that, when people get scratchy, the presenting issue is usually not the real one. I have been at meetings when huge issues have been waved through and then much time is spent on determining the price of orange squash to be sold at a forthcoming event. The relationships between the people at the meeting are generally the key. This is particularly true when you are working in a tight-knit community, where people's lives cross each other in many different contexts and no one has the authority to entirely set the agenda."* In the outer circles, there is no shortage of distractions and, before you know it, you can very easily be full-time on orange squash.

Easy wins

Tom Frawley says you can also be driven off course by the temptation to address the problem which is solvable rather than the one that matters: *"The temptation is greater the further you go out, and the more unfathomable the problems become. Mostly, people will start with the easier end of the spectrum to change and then work back. By the time they get to the really hard problems, they are exhausted and out of money, and the visionary with the energy to drive it has moved on because of their early success."* Tom says this happens time and again in the health sector.

Over-complicating

You can become unclear about your role itself in the outer circles. As Pam Chesters says: *"Some people say that, in the outer circles, you have to produce not only the question but the answers too, as you do in the core circle. But often, it's more about asking the question. It's not that there is anything wrong with producing the answers, but it's not the only way. For example, our political system militates against politicians taking unpopular decisions now, to resolve problems that will only manifest themselves in the future. Solving a pensions issue that will be acute in 20 years may be important, but can be problematic if your immediate response causes you to be booted out of office. Politicians are much more likely to address long-term issues if society is shouting about them: then it becomes more possible and it won't be one party alone addressing them. So leaders need to be asking the questions and creating a momentum around them."*

So, lots of things can blow you off course. To spot them and negotiate them, you need an ear to the ground – and strong, diverse networks. Oliver Nyumbu is Chief Executive of Caret Ltd, a business consultancy. He gave me some good advice: *"You need sometimes to be on the dance floor, and sometimes on the balcony above. On the floor, you get the smell, the beat, the rhythm, the energy. On the balcony, you see the patterns, the smoke, the gaps, and the whole picture."*

THE RIGHT METHOD 2: THE LONG GAME

Whether you like it or not, leading beyond authority is a long game. Leaders who try to speed it up with a quick decision (as Stranger Two said, like the alcoholic who slips back) are doomed to fail. It has to be a long game because the issues are not simple. They are interconnected and interdependent and there are many, many players involved. Sure, there may be some quick opportunities that demand that you move fast and free, but they will be unusual. The majority will be long games. Maeve Sherlock is Chief Executive of the Refugee Council, dealing with many of our most intractable problems. She used to be a Special Advisor at the Treasury. She says it was no fun being interviewed by the media about issues she was working on because the truthful (but, to most people, unsatisfactory) answer to most questions was always: *"It will need to be multi-agency, working over a long period of time, and the results will be hard to see."*

The fact that there are few quick fixes is not motivating. And it is truest of the things that matter the most. Tom Frawley agrees: *"There is no such thing as rapid change – it's an illusion. People are obsessed with step change. They underestimate how few people really understand the need for change. They will take a lot of persuading most of the time. To produce it, you have to go relentlessly at it, and push for it, over a long period of time."*

Patience

Janet Gaymer calls it "the long march." She says: *"Looking back after five years as senior partner, as ever you think of all the things you set out to achieve and didn't. Mainly it was because you underestimated the timescales. Pretty well everything takes a long time, except where there is a 'burning platform' which facilitates immediate change."* Simon Fanshawe met Bruce Kent, the legendary anti-nuclear activist, on a train once. He asked him what it felt like to have lost the battle. Bruce Kent replied: *"Lost? There is no possibility now of having a debate on nuclear weapons without unilateral disarmament being one of the poles of the debate. We changed the parameters. I call that winning."*

David Puttnam agrees about long games. He reckons that he made the transition to the outer circles more easily as a businessman because of the sector he was in: *"Making films calls for endless patience. The Killing Fields (which was the best movie I ever made), took me four and a half years from reading the script to attending the premiere. You have to get used to waiting for scripts, then waiting for rewrites, and then waiting for decisions.* Chariots of Fire *took three years – and a stream of insulting letters (some of which I then framed just to remind me). I am very patient. If I get blocked off here, I'll try something different there, but I will always come back. Someone once said of me: 'Don't waste your time saying no to him.' Maybe he did not mean it as a compliment, but I took it as one."*

Waiting – but ready

Timing is crucial. Sir Cyril Chantler is the Chair of Great Ormond Street (the internationally renowned London hospital for children). He told me a story that illustrates this: "*Following a year in the USA working with hospitals and researchers, I returned to London in 1972 with ideas for services to children in the UK. I got together with two colleagues to see if we could come up with a solution to the problem of caring for children with renal failure – which is both rare and complicated. We consulted pediatricians, specialists, doctors who dealt with adults and we produced a plan, properly worked through, to sort out the problem. It was to set up eight centers of excellence in England, two in Scotland, one in Wales, and one in Northern Ireland. The Department of Health did not think the time was right and the plan was shelved.*

In 1979, Mrs Thatcher was interviewed on television about the Health Service. She said that there were plans to set up a national service for adults with bone marrow disease. This was news to the Department of Health, who then felt they needed some kind of plan to make these promises materialize. The next day, our plan was dusted off – and it was all there, all worked out. Our plan formed the backbone for national services across the UK."

This is an approach I have used quite a few times now, albeit in operations on a smaller scale – to bide your time but to be there with an answer, worked through and ready to go. One of my father's favorite stories was about Mummy and Daddy rabbit eating in the garden when the farmer comes out. Daddy rabbit rushes down the nearest hole with Mummy in hot pursuit, leaving the farmer standing over it. Mummy rabbit says to Daddy rabbit: "*So what do we do now?*" And he replies: "*Stay down here 'til we outnumber them.*"

I spoke to a group of peers who know the House of Lords inside out and asked them how they thought change was brought about there. They reflected on four big issues that they well remembered neither the House of Lords nor the House of Commons wanted to act on at the time: IVF, the age of consent, tobacco, and assisted dying. What had forced these issues onto the agenda? A small, committed, and co-ordinated group of people producing pressure from the outside. Two or three determined fifth columnists on the inside. And the stamina from both groups to keep on, and on, and on, putting them on the agenda until they eventually had to be addressed.

Being there

Paddy Ashdown's response to my question about why he took on the task in Bosnia, continues to resonate: "*I knew Bosnia and loved it. Enough so that I was prepared to be patient.*" David Simon would agree: "*Mostly, it's about being there. Being there, being there again, committing, keeping going, being passionate, coming again, being resilient, keeping a muscular mind, and caring a lot. The best ones are the ones that stay at the table the longest and will see things through.*" He quotes Woody Allen: "*90 percent of life is just about being there.*"

Back to the House of Lords. Susan Hitch (Manager, Lord Sainsbury's Trust), describes watching a fantastic leader beyond his authority. He used a strategy borrowed from the infantry. If you have an army on the march, you need to send people ahead to lay out the camping ground and "peg it." When the soldiers arrive, they still have to put up the tents – but everything is all ready for them. He used this pegging analogy when planning a campaign in the House. He would start by calling in all the favors he had done for other people over the years (Gill Morgan's "pennies"), and ask all those people to be at a certain debate he felt passionately about. They were to come whether they were for it or against it. He wanted, and needed, both sides to be there. There would then be a debate, considering all the pros and cons. His side would lose it (as expected), and get the text into *Hansard*, which records all parliamentary debates. All would go quiet for a while. Then, a few months later, he would cause it all to happen again. But, this time, all the arguments would have been very eloquently made already. Now it's really about voting on the question, not preparing views. Over time, he would lay out all the pegs, get the debate out there, keep it in circulation, keep coming back to it, and sometimes real change would emerge as people ran out of fresh things to say against it.

Siobhan Davies is the Artistic Director and Choreographer at Siobhan Davies Dance. She raised the money for, built, and then opened a most extraordinary space for ballet dancers where they can meet and create and dance in south London. She says it may be about being there, but it's also about *"sheer obstinacy and willfulness."*

Setting the pace

You have to get the pace right too. I sat with Janet Paraskeva, and tried to learn from her experience at the Law Society in leading change in the legal profession. As she says: *"It's all about pace, keeping going, sometimes slowing down to make sure people are with you, but never losing momentum, and never going backwards. Usually, the people in the way are an obstacle, rather than a vehicle moving in the opposite direction. An obstacle can hurt you, or delay you, but it has no energy. It's just a bunch of people saying 'no.' Whereas an oncoming vehicle will probably kill you. If you're the one with the energy and the pace, there is unlikely to be an orchestrated response which might be more difficult to overcome. The expression I use all the time is 'Just run on by.'"*

I suspect she is bloody-minded about keeping up the pace. She clearly does not let not knowing all the facts get in her way either: *"It is better not to know fully what you are letting yourself in for. It is best just to know enough so that you know if you are excited by things and if they are worth doing."*

She has a very strong rubbish detector and won't let people blind her with science (or anything else). She knows her weaknesses and finds cover for them amongst her coalition. She says, for example, that she is not intellectually clever, so has people around her who are. She does not defer to what she calls "notional" seniority, or people who only appear to be in authority and are saying no. She forces people to catch up with her, she will go slower but she won't go back, and hardly ever takes the easy option of going sideways. When she is tripped up, or trips herself up, she gets back up, or the people she has chosen to have around her push her back up. She seldom lets herself get upset by people who are not happy to back her. She usually takes time over people she has accidentally upset in her haste, and gets things right with them so that they will come with her.

When she goes about producing change, she always builds up an empirical base first by commissioning research: *"OK, so you then consult, but it can be quite cosmetic. Because most of the really important messages will have come from the first empirical market research which you did at the start to help frame the consultation."*

She approaches all tasks backwards: working out the critical path, having decided where she wants to get to and then working back to the beginning. She knows the dangers of not breaking up a problem into manageable chunks and then taking on too big a first chunk. But she also thinks there is an equal danger of not grabbing a big enough chunk to begin with. She does not move on to the next stage unless she is certain that people cannot roll back from the one that has just been completed. She never asks questions if she already knows she does not want to hear "no" to them, and she does not read the rules if she has no intention of abiding by them.

Like the Chinese general Sun-Tzu, she doesn't mind having enemies, but keeps them closer than her friends. Not that she spends too much time on them (because enemies can waste it), but she keeps a sharp eye on them. She does not get diverted by "no" people either. In her view, they're happiest reading minutes and constitutions – and they prefer to Google people rather than actually meeting them.

Judging the pace

Pace, pace, more pace, less, different, confusing pace, inspiring pace, exhausting pace. Knowing when to push harder. When absolutely not to push. When to wait. When absolutely not to wait. When to drop things. When to pick them up. When to stamp your foot. When you really must not do any stamping, not this time. When you are driving it so hard that everyone will leave you (you will turn around and no one will be there).

I know I drive things hard and never properly stop to celebrate. I also know that the forces of inertia are strong. Common Purpose would never have got off the ground if I had not driven – determinedly and fast. In those early days, I would meet people, do my best to convince them, and tell them how exciting it was and that if they wanted to be part of it, they had better run fast because we were off. And it worked. On other things, the need has been to go slower and more carefully, threading all the loose pieces back in, and getting the details right.

Maybe though, one of the deciding factors on the right pace to set is whether the space you are moving into in the outer circle is already occupied by someone else. If, as Kuben Naidoo says: *"your outer circle, your periphery, is someone else's mid-town,"* you have to move carefully, using all the coalition-building and conspiring skills, to avoid treading on toes. Whereas if you are going into the outer circles to stake out virgin territory, you can go as fast as you like. Or, at least, as fast as you can handle.

THE RIGHT METHOD: 3 CREATIVITY AND FUN

I reckon that people will volunteer authority to all kinds of leaders, as long as they are brave – and fun. As Sue Stapely says: *"You need leaders who are enjoying things, who have energy and enthusiasm. The people you won't follow (and who very often fail if they don't have authority) are the people who look miserable and who make everything a chore for themselves and for you."* Sadly, I can think of quite a few. Decent and humble and knowledgeable and bright and everything a leader beyond their authority should be, but no fun. You have to make it exciting if you want people to join you in a risky venture, with limited rewards that largely have to be internalized anyway. Diana Parker agrees: *"People want to have fun – so you have to make it fun. Then they will want to join you, rather than stick to the other things they could be doing. This is more and more relevant these days, as fewer and fewer people feel stuck with what they're doing. They know that they can move to another job so much more easily."* It has to be fun. Especially as it is unlikely to be fun all the time.

Count the laughs

Ask yourself this: how much do people laugh at the meetings you chair in your core circle? On the whole, these are meetings people know they need to be at. If you had no authority, would they still come? How often do people do really silly things that will stay in your mind forever? I will never forget going to see the then Chief Executive of Diageo with Anita Roddick. He wanted to meet the Chair of the trustees before deciding to back Common Purpose. At the meeting, Anita told him she would rub dewberry oils all over him if he would fund us. You may think this was flirtation, but it wasn't – it was just fun. But it sticks: as a giggly moment in the four hard months I spent raising the half a million pounds I knew we needed before we started. They were long and grueling and I was pregnant (with two small children at home). There was generally not that much fun to be had. Anita made it fun.

Chris Patten takes the same view: *"Leaders need all the big words: clarity, vision, consistency, moral purpose. But they also need a sense of humor. And yes, even the ability to laugh at oneself sometimes. This is what draws together happy teams, whether you have authority or not."* The fun comes in all kinds of ways, not just offering to massage people, or giggling in meetings. Surprising people is fun too. As Seamus McAleavey (Chief Executive, Northern Ireland Council for Voluntary Action), says: *"It's fun to break down the stereotypes, to surprise people because they think they have you taped and then you do something they had not guessed you would."*

Too much rigor can restrict

A while ago, I went on a project management course with my colleagues. I found it incredibly useful. Doug Miller would have been proud of me: it pummeled in the need to clarify the objective with precision. To get its scope right. To communicate it properly. To establish "objectives" and know where we were going. To pin down the "dependencies" (all the things others need to do if you are to succeed). To establish the "milestones," so that you know if you are making progress. And to decide how you are going to "evaluate" it all at the end.

It was about method – and it was very helpful. Doing it with my colleagues reinforced the need to go through the process, so that the rest of the team knew where we were at any time, and it was not me just setting off somewhere. Not that I often do (and not that the course was full of revelations), but it was a good reminder of the need for rigor. However, as I digested it further, my sense of unease increased. Yes, all this rigor might well produce something good. But maybe this level of clarity and control would also mean we would never produce anything fantastic.

Know when to let go

For fantastic, you have to let go more. You have to go beyond a project planning approach. Because fantastic is crucial when you are beyond your authority. If people are going to volunteer authority to you, a key reason will be that they know, deep down, that this is going to be really special.

Fortunately, I met Siobhan Davies soon after the course. She is a ballet dancer (her every move tells you so) as well as running her ballet company. She said how helpful such courses had been to her when she had a delivery task to achieve but that, if it was about creating something wonderful, it took much more. In this case, the analytical approach becomes counter-productive. I went to her building in south London, behind the Imperial War Museum, and watched her work. I tried to understand how she produces a piece of dance when she does not have any authority (not that she wants any) to tell the internationally renowned dancers what to do.

Creating creativity

She explained it in the following way.
"Loosely, you have to:

1. *Start from nowhere. You have to 'trim back the brain' when it starts jumping ahead, as it tries to use ordinary thinking to plot it all out. You have to slip out of your normal, literal, rational self. You have to uneducate yourself, dropping all poses, shells, and structures.*
2. *Gather the artists. They come because they know their intelligence and bodies will be exposed to something new. They know that they will expand personally. They also come because they know they are going to contribute to making the work. As dancers get older, these two factors become ever more important to them.*
3. *Before rehearsals, you must start to work out the 'single cells' that the dancers will want to move around and explore. You want them doing the exploring – talent is much more useful when it is not harnessed.*
4. *Now you start with the first cell and get the dancers moving around it. Just at the point when you start to multiply, when there is a danger that you will go on and on, playing with the same ideas, you move to the next cell and start again.*
5. *Slowly, bunches of ideas develop. Then all the movement starts to have its own DNA.*
6. *Your job becomes to bring all the single cells together using your outside eye and make them add up. All the cells and all the energies eventually then release the idea.*

This cellular approach allows you to have lots of ideas without the burden of thinking them through, putting them in a logical order, or completing them. It prevents you from using the linear approach – the tidy approach – which tends to make you operate along straight lines with fixed points at both ends. You don't want to just work between the two fixed points which you can see from wherever you are at any one time. The cellular approach allows you to play in the more chaotic area, which is more interesting.

With bits all over the place, you have to weave, duck, and maneuver around obstacles. You have to shift and adapt and, in so doing, you become incredibly creative. It's chaos, but it's very rigorous chaos as you work something up. In a way, you are organizing the chaos, rather than tidying it. The real question is, how much chaos you can cope with? Will you panic that you can't pull it all together when the time comes to really complete it? There will be plenty of chaos if you are not working with an obedient team. If you can cope with this approach, it will produce a much deeper outcome. If you try to tidy, and seek to be in control, you tend to produce something which is lazy and predictable."

Create freedom

The outer circles are full of people who enjoy the freedom they find there. The lack of formal structure. The absence of earnestness. The sheer pleasure of developing ideas and watching them grow without the dead hand of structures or organograms to restrict the flow. It's just like the entrepreneurial spirit which leads so many people to make an idea happen by setting up their own small businesses. And it's what leaders who have been running big teams and big businesses will have to discover (or rediscover) when they move into the outer circles. Where they are likely to be leading small, fleet-of-foot operations that will need to draw on more of the creative skills and the dynamic energy that keep things going when there is no authority.

I discussed this with Caroline Whitfield, who left Unilever (where, in her words, everything seemed to be about "roll out") to become Chief Executive of Blackwood Distillers, based in the Shetland Islands. She says: *"Creativity is about allowing childlike play. Collective play, with no script and no mission briefs. Play that allows conversations to simply go. There are no decision trees; you have to let things flow backwards and forwards with ideas coming from everywhere. There cannot be any parameters to the play."* She sees a correlation between creativity and fun. You have to set the tone so that people have the freedom to play, using all their skills and really enjoying themselves. She believes that, if you get it right: *"Then things begin to conspire in your favor. Opportunities pop up unexpectedly. People offer their ideas because they enjoy the fresh air. They want to be part of something that is full of energy, and with people who are exciting. They are proud of having great ideas."*

She warns about four things:

❏ people who are constantly calling for "focus" and don't realize that it's all about juggling balls

- ❑ people who assume that, because something has worked in the past, it will work again
- ❑ bringing project managers into things too soon
- ❑ thinking that creativity is just about having the initial idea – you need the creativity right through into the execution.

Ignoring these last two can ensure that you get brilliant execution, but of something that is fundamentally substandard.

Apparently, her Finance Director often says of her way of working: *"I love it and I hate it – but mostly, I love it. Every time things seem to settle down, they get thrown up in the air again. But it does raise my game."*

There is a danger here of thinking that this is all very well for dance companies and small creative businesses, but what does it have to do with me? I can hear people saying: "I am not the creative type – and certainly not the giggly type." But, like public speaking, if you want to lead successfully in the outer circles, you will have to learn new ways. At least, make just a few changes. Because you need to be able to generate the sense of excitement that the artist and the entrepreneur can create. That is what will draw people into places that they don't have to be. And attract authority they don't have to give you.

There has to be a real sense of dynamism and energy in the air. And it has to come from the leader. Think about where this section started. Think about how it feels when you leave the office of the best leaders beyond authority: "You know something is about to happen. You don't know what and when and where – but you are absolutely certain something is about to happen."

SCENARIO: BOLD COALITIONS OR TORTURE BY CONSENSUS?

Building coalitions is a key part of leading beyond authority. How have you avoided it becoming leadership by consensus?

David Hill is Chief Executive of Ashford Borough Council and former secretary to the Royal Commission on the reform of the House of Lords. Prior to that, he was a civil servant in the Northern Ireland Office.

Leadership by consensus has got a bad name. It is not right for all situations, but it is the only and best option in some. I learnt this as a civil servant in Northern Ireland. Between 1976 and 1986, there were many, many White Papers on the issues of the province that proposed solutions. Most of them could have worked, if people had wanted them to. But they all came from on high. None had sufficient consensus built in to them.

What I learnt is:

❑ You need process. First, you build understanding by getting all the parties to spend time discussing the issues in general terms. Then you give them a real feel – a smell – of the prize available if they can come to agreement. And third, you prompt and help them to work out what compromise is required to get there and whether the balance of advantage makes it worthwhile. By spending time at the start on these three, you force people to get to know each other at a personal level, making it easier to build the "confidence in the other side" that is ultimately vital.

❑ All the way and at every stage you involve everyone. Consensus calls for compromise and people won't operate – or advocate – a compromise unless they were involved in striking the deal.

❑ You have to let the process take its time. The worst mistake is thinking that you can tell people what the consensus is at any stage. They must work it out for themselves. Your role is to create a mechanism for them to do so. The real trick is to know where you want to go but not to declare it. You have to promote engagement, give ownership, and create space. All the while, nudging people as you go. And learning and adjusting all the time.

All the while you need to keep the notion of "sufficient consensus" in mind. In Northern Ireland, we agreed that we would go with a consensus that was less than 100 percent – as long as it had the support of both governments and a combination of political parties that represented a majority of the voters overall and majorities on each side of the community. The mistake is to become transfixed by consensus and believe that you have to make it total. People don't have to be happy with the ultimate decision – but they do have to know that there is a valid way of coming to it.

Siobhan Davies is Artistic Director and Choreographer, Siobhan Davies Dance.

How do you build a coalition that produces something extraordinary? How do you keep away from ordinary consensus and compromise? How do you make sure you get the bubbling up of ideas through a coalition of energy, rather the boiling down that consensus inevitably provokes? Around here, there's an expression we use a lot: "it's something or nothing." It's about eliminating all the ordinary, in-between stuff that is no good. You have to cut it out and concentrate all the energy on stretching for the best. Then the really good stuff acts as a magnet for more. If you allow middling stuff to stay, the filler stuff, then that works as a magnet for more of the same too.

I learnt this approach through dance. And I use it elsewhere too.

When we took on the task of buying a huge building in south London to create a center for dance in Britain, we all knew that we had the possibility of creating something extraordinary. We gathered a coalition around us to make it happen. But it would have to be "something or nothing": we would not have people who would settle for average and produce more of the same. I am not good at getting rid of people, so this meant I had to be very careful who we brought in at the start. They needed to be both accurate and adventurous. Accurate so that the central idea remains clear and recognizable. And adventurous so that they don't miss possibilities.

Chris Patten is Chancellor of both Oxford University and Newcastle University, and former Governor of Hong Kong.

Coalitions, and for that matter consensus, are not that bad. They only get bad if they are seen as the end rather than the means – if they are not about advancing things. Of course, they need a clear agenda, a good narrative, and a broad body of support, but most of all, they need leadership.

And I mean real leadership: that is about shaping and changing opinion. This kind of leadership does not happen enough. Because too many leaders take the "safety first" approach, or they couldn't shape anything even if they tried, or they have convinced themselves that life is about a series of incremental developments and that to do more would risk failure.

Coalitions flounder, as do all ventures, without leadership. Too often they become caught up in the "focus group culture." You get together a focus group to decide what you think. Then you get together another one to decide how to communicate what you discovered that you think at the first one.

PART 7

Making it happen

So far, I've concentrated on what leaders need to change in themselves to get better at leading beyond authority. But, in order for leading beyond authority to become more legitimate, more prevalent, and more successful, there are also changes we need to bring about in the organizations we operate in – and in society at large.

Create situations within organizations

Organizations, big and small, need to recognize, distinguish, and develop the appropriate skills in their leaders. As Derek Higgs says: *"The development of leaders needs to seriously invest in taking them off the tramlines and out of their comfort zones."* We need to see more opportunities like the one offered to Brandon Gough in the early years of his career. This would mean that leaders would not just move from one leading inside authority role to the next, perhaps with a short stint in a policy role to do some thinking. We need to create more situations in which they have to lead actively and deliver change across the vertical structures of the organization. Granted, they are being appointed to the role, but they will not have the kind of authority that they are accustomed to – and if they resort to "giving instructions" they will not succeed.

Vince McGinlay, who so hated leading beyond authority at the end of his time at M&S, reflects back on a wonderful early experience of it there. He had the opportunity because he was chosen for it. When Lord Rayner was Chairman of M&S, he introduced the Scrutiny Program. With the directors, he would identify things that were not working well within the business (it was usually a silo issue). Then he would find one or two bright people who were going places (and were recognized as such) and give them the briefs. First, you had a month to produce an outline of your proposed methodology, and identify the "prize" were the problem to be solved. Then you had to go back to Lord Rayner, who could sanction or drop your proposal. If you were sanctioned, you then had two months to sort it out and turn the proposal into action. At the end of that three-month period, if the board agreed with you, it was implemented. Vince says: *"I was one of the bright young things, and it's then that I really learned to lead beyond my authority. It was very exciting! My brief was to sort out some issues in the supply chain."*

John Rose believes that you don't need to create the jobs – in most organizations, they already exist. But you do need to recognize them for what they are. As he says: *"We are in a joint venture in the USA with two other companies, one a consortium and one a competitor; all have very different cultures. In the chief executive role, in this sort of venture, you have limits on your authority; it is a very complicated structure and you are dependent on the partner companies for many of the critical activities. It is necessary to persuade and influence. We have to be very thoughtful about who we put into the role. The danger is that you put in the person who is available, rather than using it as a learning opportunity for the best you have."*

Allow leaders to lead beyond the organization

Organizations need to allow what Moira Wallace calls *"foreign travel."* You have to encourage a degree of foreign travel in the early days, otherwise you get "group think" among leaders in an organization. The research Common Purpose did among leaders in their late twenties who felt so disappointed by their "quarter-life crisis" indicated, that if organizations do not encourage this to happen more, the very best of their talent (who can afford to walk) would leave.

Years ago, a friend who was head of human resources at a major bank asked me for some help. He was putting together an argument on behalf of a member of staff. He knew it was a pretty forlorn hope, but he wanted to do his best for the person involved. She was a young graduate, about four years out of university, who was very able and promising and the bank had plans for her. When she left university, she had signed up to the bank's graduate scheme, a condition of which was that she accepted the need to move around the country every few years. Two years on, she was not disputing that she had committed to this, but, in her own time, she was a dancer and she had been offered a place in an amateur dance school of huge repute. She wanted to take up the offer: all the dance commitments were at the weekend and in the evenings but, if she moved with the bank, she would not be able to take up the place. The bank was not arguing that it would interfere with her work or her career, but that it broke the contract. My friend was trying to compile the case that, in this unusual situation, it was worth bending the rules, and that the skills she would acquire as a dancer would in fact be useful in indirect ways to the bank. They would develop her self-discipline, leadership, and creativity. We worked hard to make the case – and failed. They were worried about producing an exception to the rule but, more importantly, they could not see sufficient correlation between what she would learn as a top-quality amateur ballet dancer and banking. So she left.

A few weeks later, I went to a retirement party for employees in the company which my husband ran. I saw exactly the same issue – but this time at the end of the employees' careers. As the long-service awards were given out, the speeches described what the recipients had been doing over the years in their "other" lives – outside the company. One had led the Scout movement for the whole of the east of England. Another had been the treasurer of his trade union and had successfully frustrated Mrs Thatcher by moving all the union funds abroad in a very clever way. They had such enormous talents; and they had been leading way beyond their authority, quite naturally, for years. None of these skills had ever been recognized – or utilized – at work. I realized then that all organizations are brimming with people who can lead beyond their authority, but too often they do so outside the organization they work for, not inside it.

I believe that missing opportunities like this is madness. Peter Sherratt would agree. He would add that any organization has a greater hope of keeping great people longer if it allows them to do what he calls *"extended leadership."* Let them go out, as dancers, or volunteers, or school governors, or change makers in society. Of course, you need to think it through carefully and make the case well. Sometimes people say to me: *"I want to sit on a board,"* and my answer is: *"If that's what you will do, no. You can't just sit on it, with the emphasis on your bottom. You need to be part of the leadership of a critical organization that delivers to your community."* If you do this, you will become more effective as a leader – especially as a leader beyond your authority.

David Varney agrees: *"We need to stop dividing leaders into bits: a professional, a voter, a citizen, a family person. Because, if you divide people up, you dehumanize them. You go into the outer circle because it's about being human. I also believe that you can't run an organization properly if you just become a calculator and lose the human bit."*

Vince McGinlay says he found it a relief that this is already a given in the USA: "*When I went to run Brooks Brothers, I found that all the interesting people across the business community had a very different approach to encouraging managers to get involved beyond the day job. They expected their leaders to be pillars of both businesses and local communities. They saw this as the right thing to do; as powerful personal development and as something that is good for the business and the brand. Because this is common and accepted, if your business hits problems in the USA (unlike the UK), the stakeholders don't immediately start shouting that you took your eyes off the ball.*"

Develop leaders to operate in the outer circles – and recognize it

Organizations need to break out of this attitude of "they're bright, they'll pick it up" – and stop underestimating the differences between leading inside and beyond authority. Because, by failing to acknowledge the gaps, they allow people to fail and revert back to their core circle.

As Peter Sherratt says, good companies promote leading beyond authority both inside and outside the organization. And they help their people to do it and do it well. Peter mentors many, and works hard to get them to understand the idea of using minimum necessary force: "*You don't want to crash around using maximum force just because you have it. It will put people off and they won't let you lead them. I have seen many move into the outer circles and start throwing their weight around. In the core one, the fact that they were hugely intelligent counted for a lot and, on the whole, they were brighter than most of the people around them in there. But when they hit the first outer circle, and start saying 'I'm bright, I can out-think all of you,' the response from the equally bright people they meet is 'out here, everyone is as smart as you, so don't get clever with me.' In a good firm, you will get through this stage, and recognize it, and learn to start using the lightest touch possible, and you learn to let others take the credit. Then, and only then, are you giving the organization all you have to offer.*"

Gill Morgan agrees about the need to build in lateral thinking and leadership from the start: "*These days we need to develop more divergent thinkers, rather than convergent ones. Take the training of doctors. In my day, you were trained to meet the patient and, based on what presented in front of you, you made a diagnosis. Nowadays, we are training doctors to look at all the combined factors, to think more broadly about issues like housing and family. This is a big change, and a tough one, given the sheer number of information sources around."*

Matt Baggott is Chief Constable of Leicestershire Constabulary. He says you also have to build this into how you recognize leaders: *"We appraise three things in our leaders: what they have achieved in the role they have been given; how they are progressing in their individual development objectives; and what their influence looks like across the organization. Of course we have to create opportunities for people to deliver on the third."*

Sandy Forrest says we need to get on with it: *"How do we nurture these skills amongst our people? By balancing all the leadership development programs that are about styles and technique against opportunities to get out and really understand people. The trouble is that most leadership development is structured around the traditional ideas about leadership. This might be appropriate in self-contained environments (if any actually still exist) but, for many of us who operate in a world where successful achievement of operational goals is dependent to an extent on support, harmonization, and synergy with other organizations, it can be unhelpful."*

Create a welcoming culture for leaders who move out

Leaders in organizations need to be doing more to help people to lead beyond their authority. Instead of stomping on leaders who step out of their core circle, they should eagerly watch out for them and encourage them. Maybe even they should stomp on the people who give them a hard time about boundaries. We need to make leading beyond authority a more legitimate activity, and not allow it to be seen as snooping about in other people's territory. We need to do more to celebrate the successes of leaders who move beyond their core circle. Sandy Forrest says: *" As leaders, we need to be sophisticated enough to recognize those who are doing it and achieving success, even when they know they can't claim the credit, and afford them the support and freedom they need to continue."*

There needs to be lot of change – both in organizations and the people who lead them. Brenda Smith is Group Managing Director of the Ascent Media Group. She does not underestimate the scale of the change required and admits that she finds it hard sometimes: *"There is always the danger that you, as a deeply committed team leader who wants to create a cocoon of achievement, become a part of the problem and don't let your team out of the bubble."*

Education needs to change too

A lot of schools already do plenty to develop leading beyond authority skills – even if they don't know that they are doing it. Leadership opportunities afforded through sports are mainly about leading in authority skills but, if you try to get any group of young people together, you are inevitably going to exercise beyond authority skills too. The many clubs and campaigns run by young people throw them right into the outer circles. Common Purpose runs an award for campaigners. A couple of years ago, I remember the delight at meeting a young man in a wheelchair who had been deeply frustrated when he finally got his PIN number so he could use a cash machine. Somehow, this had always symbolized "grown-upness" for him. Then he discovered that the machines were placed so high that he could not reach them from his wheelchair. He would have to divulge his PIN number to his brother if he was to get access to his cash. His name is Nick Bishop – and he ran a long hard campaign to change the siting of the machines. He built his case, he got support, he wrote letters, he found out how to make his message resonate, and he kept going. He was an extraordinary example of leading beyond authority. The cash machines are gradually coming down in most banks (bar a few, which Nick loves to advertise whenever he can) so that he and others in wheelchairs can use them.

In some schools, they even talk about leadership in the classroom! Rudi Bogni recalls learning about leadership from his teacher: *"When I was ten and at primary school in Italy, my teacher used to present us with the biographies of historical personalities, from science, politics, and literature. We would be encouraged to discuss them and to talk about what we would have done in their place. We talked about Fleming and penicillin. About Manzoni and the difficulty of proposing a new language. We discussed Marie Curie as an individual scientist and as part of a partnership with her husband. We argued whether Cavour was right to risk his early political successes in the north and gamble it all again in the pursuit of the unification of Italy. Not bad for ten-year-old kids. This was education, not just training."* It was also looking at leading beyond authority.

Business schools are beginning to think more about how leaders operate outside their core circle, either as professionals or as citizens. The Skoll Centre for Social Entrepreneurship at the Oxford Saïd Business School, for example, does a huge amount to encourage and support leaders who want to innovate in society.

But the focus of most remains how to lead in the core circle. As Chris Mathias, who is helping to develop new modules of the programs for young leaders at INSEAD, says: *"We need to accelerate this change of emphasis, because too many MBAs are still producing people with a naive belief in the right answer, which is pretty unhelpful when you are operating beyond your authority. More dangerously, some give people the belief that they are better than anyone else. Beyond authority, this will actually be the cause of their downfall."*

The appointers have to change

Appointers have to ask questions about experience beyond authority when they are considering leaders for new roles that will take them into the outer circles. Too often, I meet people who have taken on a new role in the very outer circle and I cannot quite get my head around how they could have been appointed. Jan Hall is an international headhunter and Partner at JCA Group. She says: *"There is no better indicator of a leader's future success than their past success."* Yet a person who, for example, might have been very successfully running a drinks business without ever doing anything outside it, not even in the drinks industry body (if it exists), now has this major role leading beyond authority. I can guarantee that such people have already started rolling up their sleeves *"to get this sorted and fast,"* while everyone working around them is doing just that – working around them. Another useful idiot has been born. Maybe I am too harsh, but just a few questions about leading beyond authority might have been useful at the interview.

Society needs to encourage leaders to operate as citizens

We need a change in society – and a very fundamental change. We need to stop thinking about democracy purely in terms of voting. We need to recognize that democracy allows for a huge dominant space for politicians who are elected and accountable – and call the shots. This is right and proper – and it is not an easy space to be in. But there is another space, an invisible space. It's not as big – but it's vital. It lies between the state and the citizen. Between the immediate responsibilities facing each individual and the institutional responsibilities of the government. It is political, but not party political; a place where people come together and act for the greater good. Like the Greek *agora*, it's a space where citizens can stand up and be counted and make things happen because they believe in them. And it's open to everyone.

In an unhealthy democracy, the space is empty. People may exercise their votes but, other than that, they leave the decisions to the governments they elect. They are active in their private lives, but passive towards the society that surrounds them: they're sleepwalking. In a healthy democracy, the space is full. It teems with individuals, businesses, community organizations, and political groups. It is alive with energy and entrepreneurial activity. People hold institutions and the powerful to account. They oppose and propose. And, free from the short-term pressures of the election cycle, they can think and act for the longer term and the wider interest.

If we could get more people to understand the space, I think we would reduce the problems that leaders who are not elected encounter when they stand up to be counted. They might not have to deal with such a barrage of questions about their legitimacy. I was horrible to a radio journalist recently. I expressed a view about citizenship in an interview. He stared at me with that look that says: *"And who elected you?"* I leant over and said: *"That attitude does more to damage our democracy than anything else I know."*

Els Swaab is Advocaat, Boekel de Nerée, and member of the supervisory board of the Nederlandsche Bank NV. She observes the same challenge in Holland: *"The idea of leaders moving out of their core circle and building civil society is quite new in Holland. Our Dutch Calvinist upbringing comes with many sayings like 'please act normally, that is crazy enough.' So we leave our core circle only with great care. Also people are worried that others will perceive them to be 'eager beavers.' But we learn fast in Holland – and increasingly appreciate people who want to make a difference. As long as they do it in a modest and not too noticeable way – which of course doesn't speed things up or challenge mediocrity quite enough yet."*

We need to legitimize ourselves

As Jude Kelly told us at the outset, as leaders, as professionals, and as citizens we have to legitimize ourselves. We have to demand that society, and the organizations in it, stop discouraging leading beyond authority. We have to challenge the culture that brands leading beyond authority as interfering. We have to stop delegating to the great "they." Stop waiting for mandates to be handed to us. And start taking responsibility for problems which may not belong to us, but that we almost certainly witness or suffer the consequences of.

Otherwise, how will the real issues in organizations and in society get addressed? How do we create a culture where leaders stop pondering and act, and their activity is welcomed? Too often we conclude quietly "it's not my problem," "nothing will ever change," "no one will listen," "I don't want to be an interfering bore," "I've got better things to do," "someone will think about it or sort it." It would be good if more often we said to ourselves: "Maybe I should do something about this, whether it's my problem or not."

We also need more people to think of themselves as leaders. A young lady, who had hugely impressed me with her questions when I had joined one of our programs for the day, sent me an email the following week. She said that she had been a passenger on the top deck of a bus in London that morning and that there had been an accident. The driver was clearly hurt, as were a number of the passengers, and a lot of people were screaming at each other, for a variety of reasons. She said that she had sat for a moment or two, watching all this. Then, thinking of the program she had been on the previous week, she said to herself: *"I am a leader, so I had better stand up."* Apparently, by the time the police and ambulance arrived, she had things well under control. This is what we need. People to jump up, even when they are not on their own territory. And the more of them, the better.

Of course, even the bravest people have moments when they feel that, whatever they do or say, nothing will change. Whenever I find myself thinking *"what's the point?"* I try to remember something I heard a while ago. Apparently, someone once asked Boris Yeltsin who inspired him. He replied *"Lech Walesa."* Who, when he was asked the question, had answered *"Martin Luther King."* Who, when the question was put to him, had said *"Rosa Parks."* Another woman, sitting on a bus. Too tired to move.

Conclusion

If he were here now, my father would say that my days of leading beyond authority must be coming to an end: *"because you must really be losing it, if you are writing books about it now."*

I hope not.

I believe that we need leaders who can create their own legitimacy. Because they see further and wider – and maybe even deeper. Because they are not in it for themselves. Because they care for people and practice courage. Because they can express their vision in ways that resonate with people. Because they can inspire. Because they know how things work in different worlds and they can bring them closer together. Because they have not allowed their success in their core circle to corrupt them, to convince them that they are right and everyone else is wrong. Because they have learnt how to deal with complex equations, rather than shy away from them and stick to simple ones. Because, like great actors, they want to achieve great things and they will happily play bit parts in the great achievements of others too.

In the end, leading beyond authority is something you do because you want to be a better leader and because you want to make the world around you better.

In writing this book, I have spoken to many fine exponents of this art. I believe even more passionately in the importance of it now than when I set out. Not just for organizations. Not just for wider society. But for the individuals who do it. Because, if you do go outside your core circle, negotiate the complexities, develop the networks, and do it all successfully, your life becomes much more interesting. And so do you.

How to get better at leading beyond authority

In preparation

1. Draw out your circles. Think through what you are doing (and have done) in each one. Are you doing enough in the outer circles?
2. Look through your CV. Check that it highlights what you do outside your core circle. Is it presented as an afterthought? Does it highlight that you have learnt to lead beyond authority?
3. Think about your personal brand. Write it out in no more than 300 words, but no fewer than 50 (no PowerPoint slides!). Keep it with you and review it regularly.
4. Do your own 360-degree appraisal. Ask others what words they would use to describe your personal brand. When do they think you resonate and when do you fail to do so?
5. Think about the setting on your radar screen. What bleeps do you receive? What influences you? Consider your networks: do you have both support and turbulent varieties? Who do you listen to? Think about what you read and what you watch. What are your favorite websites? What communities or teams do you belong to? If you widened your radar screen a little, what other influences would you seek to receive?
6. Go to a meeting or an event that you, and others who know you, would consider it unlikely that you would normally be at. Set yourself targets of new ideas to acquire and new contacts to make. Follow them up.
7. Seek out opportunities that will give you the experience of being in a minority, an outsider.

In the organization circle

1. Identify some people who are leading beyond their authority within your organization and take them out to lunch. Offer encouragement or help – and be prepared to learn from them.

2. Discuss with your team the difference between rebels, transformers, useful idiots, and expert idiots. Think through examples you have all seen, both inside and outside the organization. Consider who among you plays which role, and in what circumstances. Tell each other the truth about when you are helpful and when you are not.

3. Watch for the right opportunity to take on a problem that is not your own within your organization. Before you launch yourself into it, see if you can build a guiding coalition.

4. Figure out who the important stakeholders are for your organization, and volunteer to become a link person.

5. Explain the ideas about leading beyond authority to your line manager, and tell him or her what kinds of opportunities you are looking for.

In the society circle

1. Check what you are already doing in the society circle. How long have you been doing it? Is it really pushing you? If you have been volunteering in a school, is it now time to join the governing body? If you have been on the governing body for years, should you move on to a more challenging school, or a different sector?

2. If you are not doing enough, apply to join the governing body of a local organization. Fill in the application forms – properly. Take the time to understand the culture. Be realistic about how fast you will have an impact. But make sure you use your leading beyond authority ability so that you do have an impact.

3. Think through your different commitments and roles: where are you a rebel, a transformer, a useful or expert idiot?

Quiz: how to check your progress

1. Would you consider taking on a project without a budget attached to it?
2. Do you step forward at a networking opportunity and actively seek to meet new people and make new contacts?
3. If someone is unfamiliar to you, are you excited, rather than put off?
4. Have you paved the way for someone who is leading beyond authority in the last quarter?
5. Do you wait to be authorized, or do you step up?
6. Is it unimportant if your job title is left off your badge at events?
7. At the end of a divergent discussion, do people nod when you summarize?
8. Have you felt a sense of panic because you were in unfamiliar territory in the last quarter?
9. Do people join your coalitions?
10. Can you avoid switching off when other people get unnecessarily offended and see things from their point of view?
11. Can you tempt people who wouldn't naturally trust you to listen to you?
12. When there is a task that will be a long haul, do people look to you?
13. Can you cope when you don't get the credit?
14. Have you worked out what your personal brand stands for?
15. Do people trust your personal brand?
16. Do people feel inspired when they hear you speak in public?
17. Have you dropped an expression from your vocabulary in the last year because you found it caused offence?
18. Have your plans been influenced by someone under the age of 25 in the last quarter?
19. Have you stopped leaving things to "them"?
20. Do you succeed when you have no authority – and people that you don't rate have?

21. Have you resisted the temptation to lead "from the head" in the last quarter?

How to score

❑ Count up the number of "don't know" answers and "yes" answers.

❑ Do it again next quarter.

❑ Compare your responses.

❑ Has the number of "don't know" answers gone down?

❑ Has the number of "yes" answers gone up?

If the "yes" count has gone up then you are getting better at leading beyond your authority.

Index: about the leaders